T0271428

Organizations, Strategic Risk Management and Resilience

Organizations, Strategic Risk Management and Resilience: The Impact of COVID-19 on Tourism aims to identify, analyse and underline the importance of having a conceptual framework designed to develop and improve the risk management and resilience for organizations, particularly during times of crisis.

In the aftermath of COVID-19, it is of paramount importance to predict the trajectory of change in consumer behaviour to help managers identify the basis of a resilience strategy to ideally respond to the current situation. In particular, the book focuses on the analysis and description of the Italian tourism sector, giving a report on how the tourism sector reacted to COVID-19, underlining the importance to adopt a resilient approach relevant for evaluating the effective impact of the pandemic dynamics and to provide support tools for decision-makers to be prepared for the unexpected and to be able to follow a smart adaptation.

The book shows the latest state of knowledge on the topic and will be of interest to students at an advanced level, academics and reflective practitioners in the fields of strategic and risk management and the business of tourism.

Patrizia Gazzola is a Professor of Management, Business Combination and Business Planning in the Department of Economics at the University of Insubria, Varese, Italy.

Enrica Pavione is a Professor in Business Management in the Department of Economy at the University of Insubria, Varese, Italy.

Ilaria Pessina is a Graduate in Global Entrepreneurship Economics and Management in the Department of Economics, University of Insubria, Varese, Italy.

Routledge Focus on Business and Management

The fields of business and management have grown exponentially as areas of research and education. This growth presents challenges for readers trying to keep up with the latest important insights. *Routledge Focus on Business and Management* presents small books on big topics and how they intersect with the world of business research.

Individually, each title in the series provides coverage of a key academic topic, whilst collectively, the series forms a comprehensive collection across the business disciplines.

The Multiple Case Study Design
Methodology and Application for Management Education
Daphne Halkias, Michael Neubert, Paul W. Thurman and Nicholas Harkiolakis

Organizations, Strategic Risk Management and Resilience
The Impact of COVID-19 on Tourism
Patrizia Gazzola, Enrica Pavione and Ilaria Pessina

Organizations and Complex Adaptive Systems
Masha Fidanboy

Managing Complexity in Healthcare
Lesley Kuhn and Kieran Le Plastrier

For more information about this series, please visit: www.routledge.com/Routledge-Focus-on-Business-and-Management/book-series/FBM

Organizations, Strategic Risk Management and Resilience

The Impact of COVID-19 on Tourism

**Patrizia Gazzola,
Enrica Pavione and
Ilaria Pessina**

Routledge
Taylor & Francis Group

NEW YORK AND LONDON

First published 2022
by Routledge
605 Third Avenue, New York, NY 10158

and by Routledge
4 Park Square, Milton Park, Abingdon, Oxon, OX14 4RN

Routledge is an imprint of the Taylor & Francis Group, an informa business

© 2022 Patrizia Gazzola, Enrica Pavione and Ilaria Pessina

The right of Patrizia Gazzola, Enrica Pavione and Ilaria
Pessina to be identified as authors of this work has been
asserted in accordance with sections 77 and 78 of the
Copyright, Designs and Patents Act 1988.

Library of Congress Cataloging-in-Publication Data
A catalog record for this title has been requested

ISBN: 978-1-032-21559-4 (hbk)
ISBN: 978-1-032-21560-0 (pbk)
ISBN: 978-1-003-26896-3 (ebk)

DOI: 10.4324/9781003268963

Typeset in Times New Roman
by codeMantra

Contents

Contents

Introduction

The aim of this book is to identify, analyse and emphasize the importance of having a conceptual framework for developing and improving organizations' risk management and resilience, particularly during times of crisis. The study underlines the importance of a resilient approach, which allows companies to seize the opportunities associated with all major changes. To develop this capacity, the role of strategic risk management is crucial and this aspect will find ample space in the book. The recent crisis following COVID-19 has highlighted the importance for companies to foresee changes on the demand side, in order to make the most appropriate strategic decisions.

Today's global business environment is dynamic and subject to continuous changes that create opportunities and threats for all enterprises. Such an environment puts pressure on enterprises to find effective ways to survive and develop. A lack of adequate preparation exposes organizations to environmental threats that jeopardize organizational sustainability and individual welfare. The recent COVID-19 health emergency confirmed the unpredictability of events that can have a significant impact on enterprises. Disasters, crises and other unexpected events have the potential to affect company management and to interrupt the continuity of activity flows, with consequences that can affect companies' profitability. In this context, to survive and foster future success, organizations need to develop a risk and resilience capacity that enables them to adequately react to unexpected events and achieve long-term sustainability.

Therefore, the book focuses, specifically, on describing and analysing the Italian tourism sector in terms of how it reacted to COVID-19, emphasizing the importance of adopting a resilient approach for evaluating the impact of the pandemic dynamics and for providing support tools for decision-makers to be prepared for

DOI: 10.4324/9781003268963-1

the unexpected and to adapt smartly. The Italian tourism sector is a worthwhile market for this study because the Italian population represents an important set of tourist consumers, and they are an important reference target for the tourism sector. Moreover, tourism is a leading sector of the economy in Italy. This book is divided into four chapters.

Chapter 1 reviews the relevant literature about the importance of having a risk management approach, represented as a critical business practice that helps businesses to identify, evaluate, track and mitigate the risks present in the business environment. The chapter addresses the topic of organizational resilience and analyses the relationship between risk and resilience as tools to prepare for the unexpected.

Chapter 2 outlines how the new novel coronavirus, COVID-19, took the world by storm and identifies its implications from social, economic and environmental points of view. The outbreak has produced a "de-globalization" process by forcing countries to lock down borders, preventing normal flows of goods, capital and humans. In these circumstances, a resilient approach is crucial in order to be able to face shocks and persistent structural changes in such a way that societal well-being is preserved and the heritage of future generations is not comprised.

Chapter 3 focuses on the description and analysis of the Italian tourism sector, giving details about the sector's important contribution to the overall economy and exploring the impact of COVID-19. Moreover, the chapter describes how the Italian tourism sector reacted to COVID-19. The chapter also highlights the growing importance that the so-called new forms of tourism (slow tourism, sustainable tourism and proximity tourism) are assuming and that the pandemic has probably accentuated. It is essential to predict the trajectory of change in tourist behaviour to help tourism managers identify the basis of a resilience strategy for responding ideally to the situation. It is extremely difficult to predict the real future trends in the tourism industry; nevertheless, to this end, the chapter tries to identify the primary trends that are expected to impact the tourism industry and, in particular, consumer behaviour. Predicting the trajectory of change in tourist behaviour is essential for helping tourism managers identify a resilience strategy for responding ideally to the situation. Successful companies, as proven during the crisis, will adapt to new consumer behaviours quickly and create a competitive or first-mover advantage in their specific market.

Chapter 4 describes the empirical study conducted to understand tourists' sensitivity to the health crisis caused by COVID-19, both before and after vaccine availability. By understanding travellers' changing propensities, tourism managers can make better decisions. The research is based on a survey that was given at two different periods of time: the first survey was conducted between the end of September and the middle of October 2020, while the second was conducted exactly one year later when new tools such as vaccines and the Green Pass became available.

The conclusion explains how the example covered in the book can have global applications for understanding the tourism sector, and it recommends that tourism operators adopt a resilient approach that allows them to adapt to rapid changes in the external environment.

1 Risk and Resilience Management in Turbulent Times

1.1 Definition of risk

The word "risk" is common and widely used today in connection with personal situations like health, investments, insurance, etc.; the collective social situations like the economy and safety of the country, etc.; and, company situations like corporate governance, business models, strategy, etc.[1] Nevertheless, while risk is well known and has developed to a certain degree of maturity, there is still no broad consensus on the meaning of this term; therefore, depending on the context, there are many accepted definitions of risk in use.[2]

In their Guide to Risk Statements, the Treasury Board of Canada suggests that "Risk refers to the uncertainty that surrounds future events and outcomes. It is the expression of the likelihood and impact of an event with the potential to influence the achievement of an organization's objectives".[3] The distinction between the event and the impact (positive or negative) is very important. We can consider the event as a situation that can influence the possibility of an organization reaching its objectives, while the impact is the potential effect of an event. A different definition of risk identifies it as the possibility of a deviation from expectations that could create damages. In this case, risk is the possibility of an event that moves away from the trajectory; this deviation is highlighted only when the loss has occurred.[4] To most people, risk is viewed as having a negative connotation. Quite surprisingly, some national standard-setting bodies, such as the International Organization for Standardization (ISO) ISO/IEC 27005:2008, also use a negative definition of risk.[5]

According to Heldman, most of us often ignore the other side of the picture and, thus, tend to think of risk in terms of negative consequences. However, while risks are potential events that cause

DOI: 10.4324/9781003268963-2

threats to projects, there are also potential opportunities embedded in risk.[6] As Hillson clearly identifies, there are two options regarding the definition of "risk".[7] First, risk is an umbrella term which consists of two varieties—risk with positive effects is known as opportunity, while risk with negative effects is known as threat. Second, the word "uncertainty" is a holistic term that can express the negative sense of risk as threat or the positive sense of risk as opportunity. The first option seems to be the current trend that is widely accepted by many practitioners and researchers of risk management.[8]

While there are several different definitions of risk, they seem to agree in terms of identifying two main characteristics of risk: first, it is connected with uncertainty; second, it has consequences. The connection between objective and risk is very important. By considering this link, the process of risk management can be used to identify risks, assess their significance and determine appropriate responses.[9] This link is also important for understanding attitudes toward risk because risks are driven by the objectives of the individual, the group or the organization in relation to the importance of the risk.

As Hillson suggests, it doesn't matter how the term "risk" is classified since the decision consists of both opportunities and threats that are equally important elements in terms of influencing project success.[10] Thus, both need to be managed proactively and effectively through risk management in order to prevent harm to a business.

1.1.1 Classification of risk

Risks can be classified in several ways depending on the impacts that the risk has on the internal and external environment of the company.

According to Harland, risks can be divided into the following types:[11]

- Strategic risk affects business strategy implementation, and it refers to the risk that usually arises due to a series of events or conditions that are unexpected, where the event can reduce the ability of a manager to apply his ideas or strategies.
- Operational risk is linked to the productivity of the company and to making products and services available in the pre-established quantity and quality. This risk is caused by a

malfunction or failure of the production process or another internal management process caused by system failures or human errors. This is one of the most common causes when compared with other types of risk.[12]

- Supply risk can adversely influence the inward flow of the different kinds of resources that enable operations to take place.
- Risk of hazard refers to a number of factors that can cause potential harm or adverse effects to an organization. It is crucial to identify the sources of risk that exist in a company and take the right steps to respond to them.
- Customer risk is linked to the risk that the quality of a product will not satisfy the customer, which can cause the company to lose its marketshare.
- Competitive risk arises from changes in a firm's external environment and from the firm's ability to create innovation and beat the competition.
- Reputation risk is the risk of a reduction in the company's profits or capital resulting from the loss of stakeholder trust due to a negative image of the company.
- Financial risk is connected to changes in the financial markets. It's a risk that is generally experienced by investors and arises as a result of issuers' shares and bonds that cannot afford to pay dividends or interest or loan principal and interest.
- Fiscal risk arises through changes in taxation.
- Regulatory risk arises from changes in regulations, such as environmental legislation.
- Legal risk is connected to disputes with actions deriving from various subjects such as customers, suppliers, state, employees, etc.[13]

1.2 Literature review of risk management

The ISO 31000 defines the risk management (RM) process as one that "involves the systematic application of policies, procedures and practices to the activities of communicating and consulting, establishing the context and assessing, treating, monitoring, reviewing, recording and reporting risk".[14] The first step of RM is to identify, evaluate and prioritize risks, which should be followed by an efficient use of the resources to minimize, monitor and control the likelihood and impact of negative events or to maximize the realization of positive events.[15]

Risk management requires analysing and responding to risks to ensure that an organization's objectives are achieved. The type and complexity of the organization should determine the level of RM required. However, risk management is being developed and adopted in several fields, including environmental studies, public safety, healthcare and enterprise management.[16] Facing the current world, with all its uncertainties, is not easy. Thus, the manager must use RMs to conduct normal decision-making activities in order to obtain a successful risk-taking approach.[17] These approaches, and their respective terms and definitions, have developed over recent years.

Bernoulli proposed one of the first definitions of risk. He used the geometric mean to measure and minimize risk by considering it across a set of independent events.[18] In his idea, the measurement of the risk is made by combining three variables: the probability of the occurrence of the "risky" event, the number of times the risky event is repeated in a delimited period, and the extent of the consequences (magnitude) that the event generates.

For Chapman, the definition of risk management is to facilitate better business and project results by providing insight, knowledge, and a superior decision-making capability.[19] Subsequently, the managerial literature has composed a definition of risk that includes both the positive and negative consequences of an event that can influence the achievement of a company's strategic, operational, and financial objectives.[20]

Due to the complexity and magnitude of the risks that companies have, the researchers consider a double classification of risks: pure or static risk and speculative or dynamic risk. The first risk is a negative-only risk that causes damage without, simultaneously, providing an opportunity for earnings.[21] Normally, this is caused by accidental events and is unexpected. The second risk goes in two different directions: it could be positive and create earning opportunities or negative and create damages. Entrepreneurial risk is of this type.

Another definition of RM is connected with the process of planning, organizing, directing, and controlling resources with the aim of achieving stated objectives when unexpectedly positive or negative events are possible.[22] Since risky events can be caused by both internal (infrastructure, business models, human resources, processes, and technology) and external factors (economic, environmental, social, cultural, political aspects), risk management is the process that aims to protect the company's assets and reduce or eliminate possible losses due to unexpected events thanks to the use of tools such as prevention, forecasting, insurance, etc.[23]

Though many authors have previously described risk only as being negative, some see certain types of risk as potential opportunities.[24]

In their PMBOK guide – a guide to the Project Management Body of Knowledge – the Project Management Institute (PMI) defines RM as the process that integrates risks into planning and management control with the aim of minimizing the probability that negative events will occur and maximizing the probability that positive events will occur.[25]

According to the Association for Project Management (APM), RM is "a process whereby decisions are made to accept known or assessed risks and/or the implementation of actions to reduce the consequences or probability of occurrence".[26]

Based on these explanations, we can identify risk management as a process with the main objective of identifying both the risks and opportunities that a project or business faces in its early stages and, then, taking action according to the appropriate response strategy in order to mitigate or utilize risks for the success of the business.

In their research, Mohammed and Knapkova found a positive relationship between risk management and performance. According to their findings, RM enables companies to stabilize their economic performance. By managing its risks well, a company can increase its chances of achieving its objectives, including financial ones, and reducing the risk of problems related to the reduction of profitability. In this way, the company will be protected and the whole industry and national economic system will benefit from it. Business failures also enthral other companies and therefore also the entire economic system is also negatively affected.[27]

RM can be used not only to reduce negative effects but also to obtain the maximum positive results that are available in a risky situation.[28]

Andersen argues that the ongoing information of all management and other employees is an essential activity for managing risks. The information process must be reliable and occur in real time in order to be useful for making decisions. Among the strategic objectives, the main ones are to defend the company from possible risks, take action before a linked event occurs, and balance the risk with the opportunities that are connected to the risks. Good managers keep in mind that the information process is fundamental, but they must also keep costs under control. Therefore, they must mediate between minimizing risks and keeping the firm's returns high.[29]

In risk evaluation, a key role is played by risk attitude (i.e., whether the decision-maker is risk-averse, risk-neutral, or risk-seeking), which, despite involving factors that can be objectively captured such as assets and income, largely depends on subjective factors that need to be understood, as they influence individuals' attitudes toward the risk concerned. Moreover, in order to apply risk management effectively, it is important for a company to develop a risk management culture. The risk management culture supports the overall vision, mission, and objectives of the organization, helping it to establish boundaries and adequate communication concerning what acceptable risk practices and outcomes are.

The National Institute of Standards and Technology and the ISO have developed definitions of risk management, and the ISO (ISO 31000) provides principles and common procedures for achieving a solid risk management program. These standards are designed to help organizations identify specific threats by providing a strong risk management process for the identification of the risks, a complete risk analysis and evaluation, and recommendations for treating risk, followed by a monitoring phase.[30]

Since risk is unavoidable, every organization needs to take action in order to manage risk in a way that can help to support its management and performance. RM programmes should be connected to decision-making processes to help organizations reach their goals by applying for such programmes at the individual activity level and also in functional areas. The integration of RM in managerial processes decreases the uncertainty in companies' management and reduces the risk of failure. It also helps to maintain the continuity of production and to protect the companies' images and reputations. RM contributes to minimizing the costs connected to the risk while, simultaneously, maximizing the profits.[31]

The principles of risk management are useful for every kind of organization—private, public, for-profit, non-profit, individual, etc.—thus, it is recommended to apply these principles to most organizations' risk management processes. The recognition of these principles is the first step towards the construction of a risk management framework and process.

The ISO 31000-2018 standard, Risk Management Guidelines, lists the following eight principles of risk management (see 31000-2018, Section 4, Principles):[32]

1 Integration

RM needs to be integrated into the governance and leadership of the organization. It's an essential part of the process of direction and control.

It should also be an integral part of all organizational activities to support decision-making in achieving objectives.

2 Structured, systematic and comprehensive

RM processes should be structured and systematic to include risk identification and assessment in order to determine and prioritize risks. It should include the selection, design and implementation of possible treatments for risks, and all of the operations should be connected with risk monitoring. In this way, it is possible to support the achievement of goals and to maintain an acceptable level of risk. The last step is risk reporting, which can help to identify responsibilities and improve the process.

Moreover, a company's risk management objectives and strategies must be clear. The procedures and manuals must be clear so that the risk management process is shared by all parties involved, whether internal or external.

3 Customized

The RM process needs to be personalized to the specific needs of the company—in line with internal objectives and internal and external environments. A good RM system is based on the principles of customization and continuous monitoring.

4 Inclusiveness and transparency

To implement effective RM, it is necessary to involve stakeholders at the right time and in different ways depending on their roles. The involvement of stakeholders helps to obtain different points of view and needs to be in line with the disclosure. Sharing information improves efforts to have good risk management.

5 Dynamic, interactive and responsive to change

Today, we live in a very dynamic world, and organizations need to know how to manage changes. The RM process needs to be dynamic and able to change when the organization changes, both in internal and external contexts.

The RM process needs to support the organization not only in recognizing and anticipating changes but also in mapping them so that the organization can respond in time and in the right way.

6 Based on the best available information
   The decisions that support RM are made by considering past and present information. This information helps to anticipate the future. To be useful, past and present information must be as trustworthy as possible. The past helps companies to learn from previous disruptions, avoid mistakes and adapt their decisions to new, emerging disruptions.[33] A collaborative environment can help ensure that information is shared as soon as possible.

   Risk managers have to take into account the uncertainties and limits of the available information. Clear information for stakeholders should be available in a timely manner.

7 Consider human and cultural factors
   Risk managers are people who deal with other people or groups. Their activities are carried out within one or more cultures. Different cultures are sources of different risks.

   Risk managers need to know the human and cultural risks or their organizations and consider how human and cultural factors can influence their risk management efforts.

   It is important to discuss the authority and responsibilities of the risk management group and of the other individuals who are responsible, as well as the type of communication and interactions between risk management groups and other individuals.

8 Facilitate continual improvement and enhancement of the organization
   RM is improved as managers and companies learn from experience, which must be pursued and reinforced.

1.3 Risk management process

Managing risk requires balancing different elements and their interactions with each other. To be effective, all of them need to be balanced.[34]

Risk management process involves six basic steps divided into RM planning, risk identification, risk evaluation based on risk qualitative and risk quantitative analysis, risk response development and risk monitoring and control.[35]

1.3.1 Risk management planning

The risk management plan must be anticipated by clearly setting the company objectives and verifying their consistency with the mission, the vision and the degree of risk that the company intends to assume. During the RM planning steps for a project, it is necessary to produce a detailed plan for how to approach RM activities during the entirety of a project. Informing all stakeholders of the risks is one of the main objectives. It is also necessary to be transparent and clear to establish support and commitment to a good RM strategy. This part of the planning process is fundamental for the success of a company. If the planning is extensive and covers the most important areas, the possibilities of failure will be reduced.

1.3.2 Identification of risk

Step two of the planning process is to identify events that could negatively affect the company's ability to achieve its objectives. At this stage, the company must analyse both internal and external risks. The former is more easily controlled and influenced, while the latter is beyond the control of the company. The aim of this step is to inform the whole project team about any possible risks and their characteristics and develop detailed knowledge about them.

To better analyse this step, it would be useful to differentiate companies that have never identified their risks from those that have already mapped their risks and are continuously monitoring them. The first types are new companies or companies that have new projects or that have never implemented a risk management process. The latter are companies that, despite having a risk management process in place, must nevertheless identify new risks that could arise due to changes in their internal and external environments.

By identifying risks, all of the information about those risks can be collected through several methods and techniques such as establishing control lists that contain potential sources of risks, applying techniques to collect data (brainstorming, Delphi technique, SWOT analysis), using diagrams (cause-effect diagram, the flow diagram of system or processes, etc.).

1.3.3 Risk evaluation

To evaluate risk, it is necessary to conduct a qualitative and quantitative risk analysis. To conduct a qualitative analysis of risks, risks are ranked according to their probability of occurrence and their probable impacts on the organization, primarily focusing on risks that have the highest and most immediate impacts. A probability and impact matrix or risk breakdown structure (RBS) is often used to perform qualitative analysis, which builds a foundation for quantitative analysis and risk response strategies.

Then, in quantitative risk analysis, risks are analysed numerically and prioritized based on their probable impacts. In most cases, the risks that are prioritized in qualitative risk analysis are then again analysed quantitatively in order to more accurately establish the probability of their impacts on specific projects. Probability distributions, sensitivity analysis, expected monetary value analysis, decision tree methods, modelling and simulation techniques are used to perform quantitative analysis.

1.3.4 Risk response development

In the risk response step, different actions are taken to minimize the probable impacts of negative events and to enhance the probabilities of opportunities. When any negative events or risks occur, four typical strategies are likely to be applied in response: avoid, transfer, mitigate and accept. In a risk avoidance strategy, the project team tries to eliminate the effects of risk entirely from the project. This is most often the case when the risk may change the project objective. In a risk transfer strategy, the project team transfers the responsibility of the probable risk to third parties. This strategy is typically used if there is any financial risk in the project. In a risk mitigation strategy, the project team tries to reduce the likelihood of a negative threat from occurring by using a relevant action plan and resources. If a risk cannot be avoided, transferred or mitigated, the project team applies a risk acceptance strategy, in which it decides to do nothing until the risk appears.

In contrast, when any positive risks or opportunities occur, the four typical strategies that are likely to be applied in response are the exploit, share, enhance and accept strategies. The exploit strategy is used when the project team wants to eliminate the uncertainty of any opportunities. The enhance strategy is used when the team foresees an opportunity and wants to increase the probability of its occurrence through an allocation of resources. The shared strategy is used when the team assigns ownership of an opportunity to a third party that is better suited to managing it. The acceptance strategy is used when the team takes advantage of an opportunity if it appears in the future.

1.3.5 Risk monitoring and control

Risks monitoring and control have to be performed permanently throughout a company's lifecycle. In the risk control process, the risk response plan is executed, new risks are identified, identified risks are tracked, residual risks are observed and the effectiveness of the risk process is evaluated.[36]

The benefit of this process is enhancing the efficiency of the risk management approach in the project timeline. Various techniques and several instruments, such as risk assessment, risk auditing, variance and trend analysis, technical performance measurement and reserve analysis, are used to carry out this step.

1.4 Organizational benefits from risk management

Risk management plans are an excellent support for decision-making and, above all, for reducing future risks.[37] Having a risk management plan also helps companies from a financial point of view because it allows businesses to prepare themselves financially for the most likely problems, which increases a business's appeal to lenders. Predicting risks on the basis of a structured plan allows a company to avoid the loss of basic resources and to focus on market objectives, production, etc. Most importantly, having a preventative risk management program in place can be of enormous value when something does go wrong. Such a program should make it easier to identify the responsible party, remedy the problem in a cost-effective and efficient way, and position the organization as responsible and worthy of trust. By being proactive, companies can reduce panic on the part of their stakeholders and limit the impact of any negative events by getting ahead.

Risk management improves companies' health, integrity and resilience; there are several ways in which a solid risk management plan can strengthen a company:

* RM helps companies to identify risks that are not evident.

   If an organization wants to avoid risks, it must first know what they are, even potentially. Potential risks are crucial, above all, because they are specific for the business. If the managers know the risks, they can avoid them. Managers who know and are able to identify their organization's potential risks is able to make a plan to mitigate and avoid the effects of negative impacts. In this way, managers can choose the best decision trajectory.

- RM decreases inconsistent and inefficient operations.

  A risk management process can help companies to see how some risks could create problems of consistency and/or efficiency.[38]

  If a company always buys its raw material from the same supplier located in a politically unstable area, then that is a risk. If the supplier ends up in a difficult situation, the company cannot proceed with its production and risks major inefficiencies. To reduce this risk, the firm must either find an alternative raw material or an alternative supplier before the adverse event occurs.

- An RM plan helps to increase customer satisfaction.

  A company with efficient decision-making and production processes can avoid many risks. In this way, the company reduces the likelihood that their customers will be dissatisfied by delays, production problems, etc.

- RM provides support for the decisions of the Board of Director

  The RM planning process allows companies to obtain a remarkable collection of information. On the one hand, their systematization reveals operational inefficiencies; on the other hand, it serves as a basis for the decisions that the Board of Directors must take. Decisions based on this information helps to avoid risks that could have a negative impact on management.

- RM plans can be financially beneficial.

  Banks and other financial institutions reward customers who have a risk management process by increasing credit limits or extending loans. This is because, if a problem occurs, they are more likely to have financial coverage.

- RM protects a company's assets.

  With an RM plan, it is possible not only to identify risks but also to create a priority list. This plan allows companies to respond to the event when the risk arises, saving time, money and physical resources. Thanks to this, workers can devote more time to business activities.

- RM improves an organization's reputation.

  A company that has a good reputation is able to attract the best employees, who feel confident working for that company. Furthermore, customers feel safe because they are certain that the company will remain in business.[39]

  To have RM in the decision processes helps to reduce the risk of scandals and avoid the possible problems on the brand. It holds the company to a high standard.[40]

- RM and insurance

Insurance is one of the most important elements of a risk management plan. Having appropriate insurance coverage in place is one of the best ways to reduce the impact of negative risks on a company. All businesses should have insurance coverage according to the nature of the business and the specific risks it faces.[41]

1.5 Organizational resilience

In the wake of the international events of the last decade, such as the September 11th terrorist attacks, the Indian Ocean tsunami, Hurricane Katrina, the emerging threat of a pandemic and the concurrence of continuous marketplace changes, organizations and employees have to operate in a challenging environment that includes a workplace atmosphere of uncertainty.[42]

More and more, organizations must be ready to react to unexpected events by showing that they are reliable; therefore, managers must be able to cope not only with the foreseen crises but also with those that are difficult or impossible to predict, knowing that it is essential to be ready to face unexpected and sometimes unimaginable events. In this period characterized by uncertainty, having a resilience plan is essential for organizations when they face critical situations.[43] The word "resilience" comes from the Latin words *resilere* and *resilio*, meaning "to bounce" or "to jump back". In French, it was transformed into *re ́siler*, meaning "to retract" or "to cancel". After that, it was introduced in English as the verb "resile", meaning "to return to a former position".[44] Nowadays, resilience is considered to be the ability to bounce back by recovering from adversity in the face of uncertainties, failures or even positive change.[45]

Resilience has been historically relevant in organizational scholarship, but it has been relatively absent from crisis literature.[46] Comfort et al. (2010) propose that this state of affairs may be due to the fact that researchers have spent most of their energy exploring the causes, dynamics and aftermath of crises rather than trying to understand how organizations can resist adversity or proactively deal with uncertainty and change.[47] The researchers who study crises think that the quality of a company's answer to crisis "critically depends on the capacity to enhance improvisation, coordination, flexibility, and endurance, qualities that we typically associate with resilience".[48] This ability, according to its definition, allows companies to cope with high-stress events, difficult situations and unpredictable changes.[49] Accordingly, resilience is a skill that companies must consider fundamental because it affects the company's ability to be successful in the modern world.

Resilience has been studied in a number of disciplines and has been used to describe organizations, systems or individuals who are able to react to and recover from disturbances with minimal effects on stability and functioning.[50] In psychology, resilience is defined as the ability to bounce back and to withstand hardship by repairing oneself,[51] while in the field of change management, it is viewed as the ability to demonstrate both strength and flexibility during the change process, while displaying minimal dysfunctional behaviour.[52] Boin, Comfort and Demchak (2010) define resilience as the "capacity of a social system (e.g., an organization, city, or society) to proactively adapt to and recover from disturbances that are perceived within the system to fall outside the range of normal and expected disturbance".[53] Similarly, Hall and Lamont (2013) argue that resilient systems (society, community, etc.) are characterized by their ability to improve how individuals and groups within them "assemble collective responses to challenges".[54] Wildavsky (1988) argues that resilience is a strategy aimed at coping with uncertainty and risk and defines it as "the capacity to cope with unanticipated dangers as they become manifest, learning to bounce back".[55] Meyer (1982) used the word resilience at the organizational level, referring to the capacity of an organization (embodied in the existence of resources, ideologies, routines and structures) to absorb a discrete environmental shock and restore prior order.[56] In this context, Malik (2013) defines resilience as "the developable capacity to rebound or bounce back from adversity, conflict, and failure or even positive events, progress, and increased responsibility".[57] Collectively, these definitions suggest that organizational resilience is the ability of an organization to deal with internal and external changes and risks.[58]

A company's ability to bounce back when unexpected and powerful events occur represents its capacity for organizational resilience. Such events, if the firm were unable to recover from them, could jeopardize the long-term survival of the firm itself. Thanks to their capacity for resilience, companies are able to respond to unexpected events, and, depending on their capacity for resilience, some companies are more capable of responding effectively to disruptive shocks than others.[59]

Several scholars define organizational resilience as the organization's capacity to learn from environmental factors[60] and gain the required resources to recover and bounce back to its normal position after a disruption.[61] It has also been defined as the capacity that employees have (promoted and supported by the organization) to use resources to positively cope with, adapt to and thrive in response to changing work circumstances.[62]

The very nature of emergencies requires that organizations adopt decentralized decision-making structures, rather than relying on hierarchy and centralized authority. During crises, formal role descriptions usually no longer suffice, new procedures have to be invented and new ways of cooperation may need to be developed. Such adaptive responses require the ability to quickly transform the formal structure and to use decentralized, team-based or network approaches to solve problems.[63] Organizational resilience is also strongly affected by the relationships between its stakeholders and employees. An organization committed to building resilient employees will foster openness in communication and encourage individual contributions, personal growth and risk-taking by recognizing and rewarding employees for these behaviours.[64] Organizations need to employ people who can react quickly and efficiently to change and perceive experiences constructively, ensure adequate external resources, expand decision-making boundaries, develop the ability to create solutions on the spot and develop a tolerance for uncertainty.

Organizational resilience capacity prepares organizations to effectively manage disruptive, unexpected and potentially change by ensuring that the means needed for recovery are available, crafting creative alternatives and executing transformational change.[65]

If we compare a resilient company with a non-resilient one, we will find that the resilient company exhibits the following three main characteristics:

-    an in-depth knowledge of their situation, of the key stakeholders and of the environment in which it carries out its business;
-    greater awareness and management of its key vulnerabilities and the impact these vulnerabilities could have on the organization, both in negative and positive terms;
-    the ability to adapt to changes with new and innovative solutions and / or the ability to adapt the tools already in use to cope with new and unexpected situations.

Resilience is a function of these three qualities in a complex, dynamic and interconnected environment.[66]

Situational awareness is a measure of an organization's understanding and perception of its entire operating environment. This includes the ability to predict potential crises and opportunities; the ability to accurately identify situations and their consequences; a better understanding of the triggers of crises, a greater awareness of available resources, both internally and externally; and a better understanding of expectations, obligations and limitations in relation to the community of stakeholders, both internally (staff) and externally (customers, suppliers, investors, consultants, etc.). Vulnerability, as defined by Etkin (2004), is the propensity to suffer some degree of loss from a hazardous event.[67]

The impacts of vulnerabilities may be either instantaneous (occur suddenly and require the failure of only one component to have a significant negative impact) or insidious (small failures of key components lead to a large-scale cascading-type failure over time). It is important for organizations to also have a clear understanding of the links between components and the vulnerabilities that may arise from these. These may include specific, tangible organizational components, such as buildings, structures, critical supplies, computers, services and specialized equipment, individual managers, decision-makers and subject matter experts. They may also be less tangible, such as relationships between key internal and external groups, communication structures and the perception of the organization's strategic vision.[68]

Another important quality is the adaptive capacity of an organization, which is a measure of the organization's culture and dynamics that allow it to make decisions in a timely and appropriate manner both in day-to-day business and during crises. It considers aspects of an organization that may include leadership and decision-making structures; the acquisition, dissemination and retention of information and knowledge; and the degree of creativity and flexibility that the organization promotes or tolerates.

An organization must have high resilience in order to be able to identify and respond quickly to situations that could become crises and that could result in potentially negative consequences. It is important to be able to find solutions to minimize negative impacts and allow opportunities to be seen even in the most difficult circumstances. To move forward even in times of adversity, companies need to be able to discover opportunities.

With this in mind, Folke et al. (2003) identify four critical factors, or clusters of factors, that interact across temporal and spatial scales and that seem to be important in building resilience in organizations and other social–ecological systems.[69] These factors include learning to live with change and uncertainty, developing diversity in its various forms, combining different types of knowledge for learning and creating opportunities for self-organization and cross-scale linkages.[70] Living with change and uncertainty begins by developing adaptations to deal with disturbances, as many resilient organizations have done. Abandoning the concept of stability means learning how to live with uncertainty, mapping past events, facing unexpected events and increasing one's ability to learn from crises. It is important to create the tools and procedures to support the necessary reactions when unexpected events happen.[71]

Learning to live with diversity provides the basis for new opportunities in the renewal cycle and increases a company's capacity to deal with shocks and stresses, making the organization less vulnerable. Diversification is a universal strategy aimed at reducing risks and increasing options in the face of hazards.[72] Increasing the diversity of players has the advantage of bringing new thinking, expanding the roles of information, education and dialogue. This concept is highly related to the third factor, namely combining different kinds of knowledge together and focusing on the complementarity of knowledge systems, which can help increase the capacity to learn. Such relationships bring together parties with different relative strengths in terms of knowledge and backgrounds, such as co-management boards or the creation of platforms for cross-scale dialogue, allowing each partner to share their expertise with the company. The last factor is about creating opportunities for self-organization by strengthening institutional memory[73] and developing learning organizations and adaptive co-management.[74]

First, strengthening community-based management and building cross-scale management capabilities is necessary for facing risks in this complex world and for dealing with disasters. Second, dynamic learning capabilities are fundamental for supporting innovation and the ability to create new answers or arrangements. Learning processes can be created or improved as a result of adaptive co-management, which is the process that brings together collaborative and adaptive approaches and focuses on learning-by-doing.[75] Nevertheless, there are a number of obstacles that stand in the way of resilience-building strategies, such as the vulnerability registered by exposure to hazards, but, in this context, resilience place provides a conceptual tool to deal with uncertainty and future change.

1.5.1 The resilience architecture framework

Although resilience is approached as a positive construct in the majority of socio-ecological systems literature, some researchers have highlighted that it can be desirable or undesirable depending on the state of the system.[76] Adaptive systems can have high levels of resilience, as they have the ability to react to a disturbance. When the disturbance occurs, their adaptive capacity makes it possible to modify their structure, processes and functions in order to increase the system's ability to adapt.[77] There are also systems that are endowed with very high resilience and that are able to resist change while maintaining their own structure and processes. In this case, the system adapts to the change by tolerating disturbances and absorbing shocks. In summary, there are two different types of resilient systems for reacting to disturbances: one in which resilience is offensive and linked to adaptation, and another in which it is defensive and linked to resistance. Organizations typically manage to combine both adaptability and resistance to change.[78]

Companies, as autopoietic systems, tend to keep themselves permanently alive by regenerating the functions and the network of processes that form their organizational fabric.[79] In the literature of organizational adaptation and learning, the interchange between adaptability and resistance is already well developed, and it relates to the adoption of exploitation (i.e., improving efficiency of existing skills) or exploration (i.e., looking for new possibilities) processes of organizational learning.[80] Organizations that balance exploitation and exploration monitor their environment carefully and continuously and identify the need and opportunity to change when it presents itself, while also maintaining and evolving the key organizational capabilities. Therefore, when assessing organizational resilience, it's important to consider two critical dimensions: the "magnitude dimension" and the "desirability dimension".[81]

The magnitude dimension refers to the level of a system's resilience (higher or lower levels of disturbance the system can tolerate and still persist). Their magnitude of resilience will depend primarily on the organizational system's characteristics and its ability to interact with its environment in either an "offensive" (adaptive) or "defensive" (reactive) way and still persist. The desirability dimension refers to the level of desirability of the system's state (more or less desirable system state at its current functional level). The desirability dimension involves a system within a wider network of organizational stakeholders, which can include individuals, groups, institutions and even natural systems. The desirability of the system is linked to both internal and external stakeholders. Internal stakeholders include shareholders, employees, managers, etc., while external stakeholders include customers, suppliers, competitors, banks and other lenders, local communities and institutions that can directly or indirectly influence the company.[82]

The Resilience Architecture Framework (RAF) provides a useful typology of organizational resilience resulting from the interaction of the two previously cited dimensions by identifying the characteristics of four organizational archetypes: transience quadrant, vulnerability quadrant, rigidity quadrant and adaptability quadrant.

When examining an organizational system's magnitude of resilience against the desirability of the system's state, companies in their early lifecycle are commonly located in the transience quadrant, as they have not yet achieved high levels of stakeholder satisfaction or resilience, and they experience a highly uncertain future. To adapt to external disturbances, they implement changes in structures and procedures. These transient systems, although highly flexible, are very unstable and, therefore, may not adapt to change. Sometimes companies that are in a phase of reorganization or deep restructuring can enter this phase for a certain period of time, which can be of greater or lesser length depending on their ability to manage change while minimizing their risk of failure, maintaining a good level of resilience. In the event that there is a failure, the system may not survive; it may destroy itself or, if possible, be reduced in size.

Companies that are positioned in the rigidity quadrant usually have signs of decline that lead to their inability to meet the needs of some stakeholders. The signs of decline might include a decrease in sales, a reduction in productivity and/or profitability, a deterioration in reputation and customer satisfaction, etc. Even in the face of strong signals, the system is unable to change and reorganize itself. The reasons may be linked to a lack of capital necessary to initiate and sustain the process of change, or they may be linked to the presence of strong defence mechanisms aimed at maintaining the structure against internal or external pressures. These systems may be able to stay alive even for long periods, closed in this trap of rigidity. However, they can suddenly collapse due to an unforeseen event because they are not able to change course and reverse direction. The trap of rigidity can also be dangerous for adaptive organizations. If they stiffen by keeping only the successful strategies of the past alive, they fail to understand the conditions of a changing market. This is called "routine rigidity" because it is linked to the lack of ability to change processes and business models.

Organizations that are in the vulnerability quadrant can achieve stakeholder satisfaction, but only if they respect certain conditions—external, internal or a combination of both—that makes them vulnerable to change. Such situational dependence could be caused by the existence of internal secret relationships, such as corruption or corporate deceit, or underinvestment in other exploratory activity. Companies that are positioned in the vulnerability quadrant can be influenced by external changes that can be linked to regulatory changes, changes in technological development, changes in consumer behaviour, innovations in the capital market and labour market, etc.

Companies that are in the adaptability quadrant are able to satisfy the majority of stakeholders by attracting a high consensus. They have high levels of resilience, high adaptability and are able to exist in a changing environment. Their dynamic abilities allow them to change in response to changes in their environment, adapting, integrating and reconfiguring processes and structures as they need to.[83] These companies have the ability to assess their internal and external environments. They manage to innovate by creating a balance between exploiting existing skills and maintaining a strong openness to experimenting with new skills.

1.5.2 Behavioural, cognitive and contextual elements of resilience

According to Lengnick-Hall et al. (2009, 2011, 2016), an organization's resilience capacity is developed according to the resilience of three dimensions: behavioural, cognitive and contextual.[84] These three dimensions are interconnected and work together while having independent and completely different roles.[85] The interconnections are synergistic and reinforce each other. They each play a fundamental role in the development of distinctive skills and the ability to use resources efficiently.[86]

First, behavioural resilience is connected to an organization's behaviours and the routines that allow it to better understand a given situation, structure new routines and use resources efficiently. This is especially true when there are uncertain situations that come as a surprise and that can jeopardize the survival of the organization itself in the medium and long term. The actions taken allow managers and other collaborators to find solutions to new challenges and threats through collaboration. Behavioural resilience creates a dynamic tension between different behaviours that facilitate creativity and lay the foundation for inventiveness. Organizations become learning organizations and implement new routines or reinforce existing ones based on new ideas, conflict management and change facilitation. In this way, they are able to respond to unpredictable and new challenges.

Second, strong identity and constructive sense-making are the two most important components for the creation of cognitive resilience.[87] Cognitive resilience requires a good awareness of reality and also the ability to question models that were valid in the past but that may not be valid in the future.[88] Companies can promote a positive and constructive conceptual orientation through behaviour aimed at reinforcing the sense of belonging and the values of the company. The constructive sense is mainly based on the company's communication and image.[89]

Finally, contextual resilience provides a setting to develop attitudes and facilitate behaviours that promote a collaborative response to environmental complexities. Contextual resilience alone is not enough to build resilience capacity, but it is essential to enable the behavioural and mental models that create organizational resilience.

Ultimately, resilient organizations are able to maintain excellent relationships with suppliers, customers and strategic allies to support initiatives in which adaptive capacity is needed. This is possible when companies have resilient individuals who are able to create relationships with other subjects who represent key resources.[90] Resilient businesses are built on individual and group responsibility.[91] The three central dimensions work together to create the capacity to develop strategic agility.

1.5.3 The progression of resilience maturity

Resilience is the ability to adapt, as well as how we understand and deal with the uncertainty associated with internal and external environments. It is not just about surviving adversity. Gibson and Tarrant list a range of interdependent factors that need to be considered in the management of organizational resilience.[92] Moreover, they explain the progression of an organization's resilience maturity and explore how resilience is based on different strategies that enhance organizational capabilities. In this exploration, they consider the following key principles:

- Resilience is an outcome.
- Resilience is the reaction to a substantial change.
- Resilience is dynamic. Resilience changes as the external environment changes over time and can increase or decrease depending on contextual changes.

- Resilience is a complex of many factors. Each factor's contribution changes when the circumstance changes.
- Resilience is described by several models.
- When a company invests in improving its resilience, there will be an increasing maturity in its resilience capabilities and its capacity to adapt to conditions of high uncertainty.
- Resilience is based on a good risk management. Normally, those companies that have a good assessment, treatment, monitoring, and communication about risk have also developed a resilient approach.

Models that use a static approach to resilience are very limited since resilience arises from the interaction between the company and the internal and external environment. Organizational resilience is based on understanding risks and how to deal with them. These are primarily unusual risks and risks related to disruption. Gibson and Tarrant demonstrate which organizational attributes can help an organization deal with uncertainty and adversity and provide insight into the types of changes that an organization needs to consider making as it strives to improve its resilience. Based on their research, the following are the key factors that create resilience: a company's mission and values, trust, strong vision, leadership that is in line with stated values and strategy that includes risk management. These factors are connected with the organization's culture. The interconnections of the elements give companies the necessary flexibility to react and adapt to changing environments.

1.6 Relationship between risk and resilience

The challenge of adversity is the main goal of both risk management and resilience. Therefore, they are closely related. There are models that integrate these two aspects. Indeed, a solid risk management process is essential for organizational resilience.[93] In these models, RM is the basis of the connection between different organizational capabilities: crisis management, business continuity, emergency response and security. RM allows companies to reach a shared understanding of uncertainty arising from high volatility, and it provides the tools for facing uncertainty with specialized skills.

While RM contributes significantly to the stability of an organization, it is sometimes not enough because traditional risk management tools cannot always protect against unpredictable crises. Today's world is characterized by improbable events with complex causes. The main characteristic of many crises today is that they are triggered by unlikely events whose causes are not well understood.[94] Many crises emerge from a pattern of several events coinciding in space and time, and the joint occurrence and cascading consequences of such adverse events are hard to anticipate and predict. Traditional risk management systems are unable to deal with disruptive events like the ones we are witnessing. For this reason, industry experts are shifting their focus from identifying and mitigating risk to trying to increase resilience.

Resilience highlights the ability of a system to absorb and recover from shocks, modifying models and structures to react to a situation of long-term stress, change and uncertainty. To do this, it is necessary to know the risk scenarios, try to understand how to best manage them and place particular emphasis on those parts of the system that help address those risks. It is also important to understand how the interrelation of these parts affects the functioning of the system.[95] While traditional risk management approaches focus on identifying risks and mitigating the level of vulnerability to external events, the resilience approach is aimed at focusing on the skills and capacities that create or conserve resources in a sufficiently large form.[96]

Notes

1 Hillson D., Murray-Webster R., *Understanding and managing risk attitudes.* Aldershot: Gower Publishing, Ltd, 2004, pp. 1–11.
2 Mandru L., "How to control risks? Towards a structure of enterprise risk management process", *Journal of Public Administration, Finance and Law*, Alexandru Ioan Cuza University, Faculty of Economics and Business Administration, Vol. 9 No. 9, 2016, pp. 80–92.
3 Treasury Board of Canada, *TBS' guide to risk statements is meant to help strengthen risk management practices by providing guidance on how to develop risk statements*, 2000, p. 4
4 Susanto A., Meiryani, "The importance of risk management in an organizations", *International Journal of Scientific & Technology Research*, Vol. 7 No. 11, November 2018, pp. 103–107.
5 https://www.iso.org/obp/ui/#iso:std:iso:31000:ed-2:v1:en
6 Heldman K., *Project management professional*, Hoboken, NJ: Wiley Publishing, 2005.
7 Hillson D., "Extending the risk process to manage opportunities", *International Journal of Project Management*, Vol. 20 No. 3, 2002, pp. 235–240.
8 Hillson D., Murray-Webster R., op. cit.
9 Hillson D., op cit.

10 Hillson D., op. cit.
11 Harland C., Brenchley R., Walker H., "Risk in supply networks", *Journal of Purchasing and Supply Management*, Vol. 9 No. 2, 2003, pp. 51–62.
12 Susanto A., Meiryani, "The importance of risk management in an organizations", *International Journal of Scientific & Technology Research*, Vol. 7 No. 11, 2018, pp. 103–107.
13 Pessina I., "Risk and resilience management as a response to COVID-19 pandemic outbreak. Towards a new and refreshing approach", *Economia Aziendale Online*, Vol. 12 No. 1, 2021, pp. 27–37.
14 ISO 31000:2018, *Risk management standard – Guidelines*, International Organization for Standardization, 2018, chapter 6.1.
15 Savica D., Aleksandra S., "Risk management", *Entrepreneurship*, Vol. V No. 1, 2017, pp. 86–96.
16 Verbano C., Venturini K., "Managing risks in SMEs: A literature review and research agenda", *Journal of Technology Management & Innovation*, Vol. 8 No. 3, 2013, pp. 186–197.
17 Hillson D., op. cit.
18 Bernoulli D., "Exposition of a new theory on the measurement of risk", *Econometrica*, Vol. 22 No. 1, 1954, pp. 23–36.
19 Chapman C., "Project risk analysis and management—PRAM the generic process", *International Journal of Project Management*, Vol. 15 No. 5, October 1997, pp. 273–281.
20 BBA – British Bankers' Association, International Swaps and Derivatives Association, PricewaterhouseCoopers LLP, *Operational risk: The next frontier*. Philadelphia, PA: RMA, 1999.
21 Verbano C., Venturini K., op. cit.
22 Head L.G., *Risk management – Why and how*. Dallas, TX: International Risk Management Institute, 2009.
23 Urciouli V., Crenca G., *Risk Management: Strategie e processi decisionali nella gestione dei rischi puri d'impresa*. Rovereto: ISBA, 1989.
24 Razali A., Tahir I., "Review of the literature on enterprise risk management", *Business Management Dynamic Magazine*, Vol. 5 No. 1, 2011.
25 IBM, Corporate responsibility report 2016, IBM Corporation, 2017.
26 APM, *APM body of knowledge* (7th ed). Princes Risborough Buckinghamshire: Association for Project Management Ibis House, 2019.
27 Mohammed H.K,. Knapkova A., "The impact of total risk management on company's performance", *Procedia – Social and Behavioral Sciences*, Vol. 220, March 2016, pp. 271–277.
28 Essinger J., Rosen J., *Using technology for risk management*. First published. England: Woodhead-Faulkner, 1991.
29 Andersen T.J., "The performance relationship of effective risk management: Exploring the firm-specific investment rationale", *Long Range Planning*, Vol. 41, 2008, pp. 155–176.
30 ISO 31000:2018, *Risk management guidelines*. Available at: https://pecb.com/whitepaper/iso-310002018-risk-management-guidelines
31 Urciouli V., Crenca G., op. cit.
32 ISO 31000:2018, op. cit.
33 Peche R.J., Oakley K.E., "Hormesis: An evolutionary 'predict and prepare' survival mechanism", *Leadership & Organisation Development Journal*, Vol. 26 No. 8, 2005, pp. 673–687.

34 Hillson D., op. cit.; Jurisch M.C., Rosenberg Z., Krcmar H., "Emergent risks in business process change projects", *Business Process Management Journal*, Vol. 22 No. 4, 2016, pp. 791–811.

35 Crovini C., Santoro G., Ossola G., "Rethinking risk management in entrepreneurial SMEs: Towards the integration with the decision-making process", *Management Decision*, Vol. 59 No. 5, 2021, pp. 1085–1113.

36 Kululanga G., Kuotcha W., "Measuring project risk management process for construction contractors with statement indicators linked to numerical scores", *Engineering, Construction and Architectural Management*, Vol. 17 No. 4, 2010, pp. 336–351.

37 Ritchie L.E., *Building a proactive risk management program*, Risk Management & Crisis Response, October 2014.

38 Kedir H., Knapkova A., "The impact of total risk management on company's performance", *Social and Behavioral Sciences*, Vol. 220, 2016, pp. 271–277.

39 Hsu L., Fournier S., Srinivasan S., "Brand architecture strategy and firm value: How leveraging, separating and distancing the corporate brand affects risk and returns", *Journal of the Academy of Marketing Science*, Vol. 44 No. 2, 2016, pp. 261–280.

40 Jafari M., Chadegani A.A., Biglari V., "Effective risk management and company's performance: Investment in innovations and intellectual capital using behavioral and practical approach", *Journal of Economics and International Finance*, Vol. 3 No. 15, December 2011, pp. 780–786.

41 Sawalha I.H.S., "Managing adversity: Understanding some dimensions of organizational resilience", *Management Research Review*, Vol. 38 No. 4, 2015, pp. 346–366.

42 Berkes F., "Understanding uncertainty and reducing vulnerability: Lessons from resilience thinking", *Natural Hazards*, Vol. 41, 2007, pp. 283–295.

43 Kantur D., İşeri-Say A., "Organizational resilience: A conceptual integrative framework", *Journal of Management & Organization*, Vol. 18 No. 6, 2012, pp. 762–773; Lengnick-Hall C. et al., "Developing a capacity for organizational resilience through strategic human resource management", *Human Resource Management Review*, Vol. 21, 2011, pp. 243–255.

44 Williams T.A. et al., "Organizational response to adversity: Fusing crisis management and resilience research streams", *Academy of Management Annals*, Vol. 11 No. 2, 2017, pp. 733–769.

45 Luthans F., "The need for and meaning of positive organizational behavior", *Journal of Organizational Behavior*, Vol. 23, 2002, pp. 695–706.

46 Boin A., et al., "The rise of resilience", in Comfort L.K., Boin A., Demchak C.C. (Eds.), *Designing resilience: Preparing for extreme events*. Pittsburgh, PA: University of Pittsburgh Press, 2010, pp. 1–12.

47 Comfort L.K. et al., "Resilience, entropy, and efficiency in crisis management", *Risk, Hazards, & Crisis in Public Policy*, Vol. 12, January 2010.

48 Boin A. et al., op. cit.

49 McManus S., Seville E., Vargo J., Brunsdon D., "Facilitated process for improving organizational resilience", *Natural Hazards Review*, Vol. 9, 2008, pp. 81–90.

50 Linnenluecke M.K., "Resilience in business and management research: A review of influential publications and a research agenda", *International Journal of Management Reviews*, Vol. 19, 2015, pp. 4–30; Sutcliffe K.M., Vogus T.J., "Organizing for resilience", in Cameron K.S., Dutton J.E., Quinn R.E. (Eds.), *Positive organizational scholarship: Foundations of a new discipline.* San Francisco, CA: Berrett-Koehler, 2003, pp. 94–110.

51 Higgins G.O., *Resilient adults: Overcoming a cruel past.* Jossey-Bass, 1994; Wolin S.J., Wolin S., *The resilient self: How survivors of troubled families arise above adversity*, New York: Villard Books, 1993.

52 Conner D.R., *Managing at the speed of change: How resilient managers succeed and prosper where others fail.* New York: Villard Books, 1993.

53 Boin A. et al., op. cit.

54 Hall P.A., Lamont M., *Social resilience in the neoliberal era.* Cambridge: Cambridge University Press, 2013.

55 Wildavsky A.B., *Searching for safety* (Vol. 10). New Brunswick, NJ: Transaction Publishers, 1988.

56 Meyer A.D., "Adapting to environmental jolts", *Administrative Science Quarterly*, Vol. 27 No. 4, 1982, pp. 515–537.

57 Malik A., "Efficacy, hope, optimism and resilience at workplace – Positive organizational behavior", *International Journal of Scientific and Research Publications*, Vol. 3 No 10, October 2013.

58 Rathina Velu S., Gopinathan S., Raman M., "Competency assessment for OR-COVID-19", *Journal of Humanities and Social Sciences Research*, Vol. 2 No. S, 2020, pp. 111–130.

59 Lengnick-Hall C.A., Beck T.E., "Resilience capacity and strategic agility: Prerequisites for thriving in a dynamic environment", Working Papers 0059, College of Business, University of Texas at San Antonio, 2009.

60 Limnios E.A.M., Mazzarol T., Ghadouani A., Schilizzi S., "The resilience architecture framework: Four organizational archetypes", *European Management Journal*, Vol. 32 No. 1, 2014, pp. 104–116.

61 Mafabi S., Munene J.C., Ahiauzu A., "Creative climate and organisational resilience: The mediating role of innovation", *International Journal of Organizational Analysis*, Vol. 23 No. 4, 2015, pp. 564–587.

62 Näswall K., Kuntz J., Hodliffe M., Malinen S., Employee Resilience Scale (EmpRes): Technical Report, Resilient Organisations Research Report, University of Canterbury. Management, Marketing, and Entrepreneurship, 2013.

63 Van der Vegt G.S., Essens P., Wahlström M., George G., "Managing risk and resilience", *Academy of Management Journal*, Vol. 58 No. 4, 2015, pp. 971–980.

64 Van der Vegt G.S., Essens P., Wahlström M., George G., op. cit.

65 McCann J., "Organizational effectiveness: Changing concepts for changing environments", *Human Resource Planning*, New York, Vol. 27 No. 1, 2004, pp. 42–50.

66 Mcmanus S., Seville E., Brunsdon D., Vargo J., "Resilience management: A framework for assessing and improving the resilience of organisations", *Resilient Organ*, 2007/01, p. 79.

67 Etkin D., Haque E., Bellisario L., Burton I., *An assessment of natural hazards and disasters in Canada*. The Canadian Natural Hazards Assessment Project, Public Safety and Emergency Preparedness Canada and Environment Canada, Ottawa, 2004.
68 Mcmanus S., Seville E., Brunsdon D., Vargo J., op. cit.
69 Folke C., Colding J., Berkes F., "Building resilience and adaptive capacity in social–ecological systems", in Berkes F., Colding J., Folke C. (Eds.), *Navigating social–ecological systems*. Cambridge: Cambridge University Press, 2003, pp. 352–387.
70 Berkes F., op. cit.
71 Hewitt K., A synthesis of the symposium and reflection on reducing risk through partnerships. Paper presented at the conference of the Canadian Risk and Hazards Network (CRHNet), November 2004, Winnipeg.
72 Turner B.L., Kasperson R.E., Matson P.A. et al., "A framework for vulnerability analysis in sustainability science", *Proceedings of the National Academy of Sciences of the United States of America*, Vol. 100, 2003, pp. 8074–8079.
73 Folke C., Hahn T., Olsson P., Norberg N., "Adaptive governance of social–ecological systems", *Annual Review of Environment and Resources*, Vol. 30, 2005, pp. 441–473.
74 Olsson P., Folke C., Berkes F., "Adaptive co-management for building resilience in social–ecological systems", *Environmental Management*, Vol. 34, 2004, pp. 75–90.
75 Folke C., Carpenter S., Elmqvist T., Gunderson L., Holling C.S., Walker B., et al., *Resilience and sustainable development: Building adaptive capacity in a world of transformations*. International Council for Science, ICSU Series on science for sustainable development No. 3, 2002, http://www.sou.gov.se/mvb/pdf/resiliens.pdf.
76 Carpenter S., Walker B., Anderies J.M., Abel N., "From metaphor to measurement: Resilience of what to what?", *Ecosystems*, Vol. 4, 2001, pp. 765–781; Derissen S., Baumgärtner S., Quaas M., "The relationship between resilience and sustainable development of ecological-economic systems", *Ecological Economics*, 2010.
77 Limnios E.A.M., Mazzarol T., Ghadouani A., Schilizzi S., op. cit.
78 Mazzarol T., Mamouni L., Resilient organizations: Offense versus defense. In Paper submitted for the Australia and New Zealand Academy of Management (ANZAM) Annual Conference, Wellington, December 2011, pp. 7–9.
79 Maturana, H.R., Varela, F.J., "Problems in the neurophysiology of cognition", in *Autopoiesis and cognition*. Dordrecht: Springer, 1980, pp. 41–47.
80 March J.G., "Exploration and exploitation in organizational learning", *Organization Science*, Vol. 2 No. 1, 1991, pp. 71–87; March J.G., Weil T., *On leadership*. Malden, MA: Blackwell Publishing, 2005.
81 Limnios E.A.M., Mazzarol T., Ghadouani A., Schilizzi S., op. cit.
82 Lawrence P.R., Lorsch J.W., "Differentiation and integration in complex organizations", *Administrative Science Quarterly*, Vol. 12 No. 1, 1967, pp. 1–47.
83 Limnios E.A.M., Mazzarol T., Ghadouani A., Schilizzi S., op. cit.

Risk Management in Turbulent Times 31

84 Lengnick-Hall C.A., Beck T.E., Lengnick-Hall M.L., "Developing a capacity for organizational resilience through strategic human resource management", *Human Resource Management Review*, Vol. 21 No. 3, 2011, pp. 243–255.

85 Hollnagel E., Nemeth C.P., eds. *Resilience engineering perspectives, Volume 2: Preparation and restoration*. CRC Press, 2016.

86 Lengnick-Hall C.A., Beck T.A., Resilience capacity and strategic agility: Prerequisites for thriving in a dynamic environment, Working Papers 0059, 2009.

87 Lengnick-Hall, C.A., Beck, T.E., "Resilience capacity and strategic agility: Prerequisites for thriving in a dynamic environment", in *Resilience engineering perspectives*. CRC Press, 2016, Vol. 2, pp. 61–92.

88 Lengnick-Hall C.A., Beck T.A., op. cit.

89 Lengnick-Hall C.A., Beck T.E., Lengnick-Hall M.L., "Developing a capacity for organizational resilience through strategic human resource management", *Human Resource Management Review*, Vol. 21 No. 3, 2011, pp. 243–255.

90 Weick K.E., "The collapse of sensemaking in organizations: The Mann Gulch disaster", *Administrative Science Quarterly*, Vol. 38 No. 4, 1993, pp. 628–652.

91 Morgan G., *Images of organization* (2nd ed.). Thousand Oaks, CA: Sage Publication Inc., 1997.

92 Gibson C., Tarrant M., "A 'conceptual models' approach to organisational resilience", *Australian Journal of Emergency Management*, Vol. 25 No. 2, 2010, pp. 6–12.

93 Williams T.A., Gruber D.A., Sutcliffe K.M., Shepherd D.A., Zhao E.Y., "Organizational response to adversity: Fusing crisis management and resilience research streams", *Academy of Management Annals*, Vol. 11 No. 2, 2017, pp. 733–769.

94 Belobrov A., "Resilience as a critical success factor of risk management", *Risk in Contemporary Economy*, Vol. 1 No. 1, 2014, pp. 325–330.

95 Van der Vegt G.S., Essens P., Wahlström M., George G., "Managing risk and resilience", *Academy of Management Journal*, Vol. 58 No. 4, 2015, pp. 971–980.

96 Vogus T.J., Sutcliffe K.M., "Organizational resilience: Towards a theory and research agenda", *2007 IEEE International Conference on Systems, Man and Cybernetics*, 2007, pp. 3418–3422.

2 Resilience Management during the Pandemic Outbreak of COVID-19

2.1 An overview of the pandemic outbreak

The fear of pandemic outbreaks is not only contemporary; people have always had to fear deadly pandemics. Rather than focusing on whether there will be an outbreak, when new outbreaks will happen is the primary concern.[1] The real problem with influenza pandemics is that they are unforeseeable but recurring events that can negatively affect societies worldwide.[2] They cannot be prevented because they are naturally recurring biological phenomena. There have been several significant disease outbreaks and pandemics recorded in human history, including the Spanish Flu, the Hong Kong Flu, severe acute respiratory syndrome (SARS) and Ebola.[3] Each pandemic adversely affected human life and economic progress. For example, the Spanish Flu pandemic of 1918–1919 killed more than 20 million people worldwide and has been seen as the most catastrophic epidemic in recorded world history.[4]

Pandemic-related crises are associated with huge negative impacts on the health, economy, society and security of national and global communities; likewise, they have generated considerable political and social disorder. Although society has been hit by several pandemics in the past, it is not easy to estimate the long-term economic, behavioural, or societal consequences because these aspects have not been received considerable attention in the past. In the limited existing studies, it is possible to find evidence that the major historical pandemics of the last century have been associated with consequent low returns on assets.[5] For a period of time after a pandemic, society tends to become less interested in investing and more interested in sparing capital, which negatively influences economic growth.[6] All society can do is take preventive measures to be able to act quickly and strive to learn from the repercussions of pandemic outbreaks to be prepared for when it happens again.

DOI: 10.4324/9781003268963-3

The Dictionary of Epidemiology features the simple but internationally accepted and renowned definition of a pandemic: "an epidemic occurring worldwide, or over a very wide area, crossing international boundaries and usually affecting a large number of people".[7] The WHO's standard definition of an influenza pandemic identifies it as a situation in which a new and highly disease-causing viral subtype that many members of the population are not immune to and that is clearly transmissible between humans establishes a base in the human population and rapidly sprawls worldwide.[8] Although there are differing definitions of the term "pandemic", it is possible to analyse some key aspects of a pandemic to obtain a comprehensive view of the concept.[9]

The first common characteristic is the geographic extension—i.e., the term pandemic is commonly used to indicate diseases that widen over large geographic territories. Indeed, a recent review of the history of influenzas pandemic classified pandemics as cross-regional and global.[10] Besides their geographic expansiveness, most uses of the term "pandemic" often include unexpected disease movement or diffusion through a transmission that can be followed from place to place. Another aspect is a novelty, since the term has been used to designate illness that is new, or at least associated with novel alternatives of organisms that already exist. Novelty, however, is a relative concept, as there have been seven cholera pandemics throughout the past 200 years, probably all caused by a variation of the same organism.[11] The fourth common aspect of a pandemic is its severity. The term is applied much more commonly to severe or deadly diseases (such as the Black Death, HIV/AIDS and SARS) than to modest diseases. Pandemics are also characterized by high rates of attack and explosive diffusion. If the transmission is non-explosive, even if it is wide-spreading, this situation will not be categorized as a pandemic. Diseases with low rates of transmission or low rates of symptomatic disease are seldom classified as pandemics, even when they disseminate extensively. The last common aspect is infectivity and contagiousness: pandemic diseases are passed from one person to another person directly (person to person) or indirectly (person to vector to person).[12]

In the past, we have observed that infectious disease epidemics do not recognize borders; they travel with people. In a globalized society, they are capable of threatening the economic stability of a country, a region, or the entire world.[13] In addition to problems related to health, sometimes even leading to death, pandemics also have important negative consequences in the social, economic and political realms.[14] For example, "[t]he impact of pandemic influenza in 2009 was not just on mortality, but also on health-care systems, animal health, agriculture, education, transport, tourism and the financial sector".[15] Moreover, the Ebola pandemics of 2013 and 2015 affected the economies and social orders in China and West Africa. Causing death and illness, Ebola and other pandemics have dramatically decreased the quality of life for families and communities and disrupted important services, including education, tourism and transport. This caused West African economies to shrink and led to the isolation of populations, which had impacts outside of Africa too due to the global attempt to contain the outbreak.[16] Ultimately, pandemics have affected billions of people, causing universal severe illness in big populations and thousands of deaths. Therefore, they represent a danger and risk—not only to individual populations around the world but also to the stability of the global economy and the maintenance of society.

2.2 A review of COVID-19 impact on the overall economy

The outbreak of the novel coronavirus COVID-19 (also known as SARS-CoV-2) took the world by storm, having a big impact on economies all over the world.[17] The "fast globalization" of the coronavirus pandemic is something that the world had never experienced before.[18] The first COVID-19 infections were reported in December 2019 in Wuhan, the seventh-largest city in China. The outbreak of the pathogen was localized to a regional seafood market in Wuhan, which was closed by local authorities on January 1, 2020, immediately after they declared an epidemiological alert. At that time, 41 people were already infected.[19] Initial investigations concluded that the infections were caused by a novel virus that could be transmitted person-to-person.[20] The novel coronavirus (now referred to as COVID-19) is an acute infectious respiratory disease passed from person to person through contact with respiratory droplets. COVID-19 can cause fever, cough, and breathing problems; in severe cases, it causes pneumonia, acute breathing syndrome, heart failure, and sometimes even death.

On January 21, 2020, the World Health Organization (WHO) published its first statement on the coronavirus situation, confirming 282 cases in 4 countries, including China (278 cases), Thailand (2 cases), Japan (1 case) and the Republic of Korea (1 case).[21] Three days later, the first European cases of the coronavirus were added to the WHO's reporting. Subsequently, on January 30, 2020, after the spread of the virus in China and its first presentation in other parts of the world, the newly created emergency commission proclaimed the new coronavirus a public health emergency of international concern since local outbreaks can quickly spread worldwide thanks to international mobility.[22] Initially, China was the epicentre with a very high number of infections and deaths, but that growth rapidly spread to Europe, where Italy became the next epicentre.[23] In March, about 120,000 cases were verified around the world, and the WHO's General Director identified COVID-19 as a "pandemic" (WHO, 2020), meaning a worldwide epidemic affecting a huge number of people across boundaries.

The declaration of COVID-19 as a pandemic acknowledged the importance and threat of the virus. The number of infected cases and the number of deaths were both increasing very quickly. There were a total of 285 million confirmed cases worldwide from January 23, 2020 to December 31, 2021 according to Coronavirus Statistics of Wordometer.[24] Moreover, in the same period, the number of COVID-19 deaths confirmed by Ourworlindata,[25] is approximately 5,420,000. Considering the features of modern medicine like state-of-the-art hospitals and infectious disease research centres, the number of infected persons involved has been incredibly high compared to other similar outbreaks in the past.[26]

The COVID-19 outbreak is causing direct and indirect economic impacts across countries, although it may be too early to identify all of the details. The outbreak seems to have produced a "deglobalization" process, forcing countries to lock their borders down to avoid flows of goods, capital and humans. As a result, many businesses and production lines have been forced to close temporarily.

The COVID-19 outbreak is also causing alarming health consequences and is resulting in enormous economic burdens for many nations, including China, the US, Japan, Germany, Britain, France and Italy – the G7 countries. Baldwin and di Munro[27] also confirm that the pandemic has affected all major economies, including those of G7 countries. Taken together, these countries cover 60% of world supply and demand (GDP), 65% of world production and 41% of world manufacturing exports. Unfortunately, these severely affected economies will drag the other economies connected to them into the crisis.

The consequences of this global pandemic are huge, and countries will considerably be affected, in particular, because of the simultaneous demand and supply shock, where demand decreases as consumers reduce their purchasing of non-essential goods and services like travel and leisure,[28] while supply is defeated because many companies are not prepared to face the phenomenon of disrupted supply chains.[29] Consequently, many service and manufacturing sectors have had to close their operations.[30] Moreover, to prevent, or at least weaken, the spread of COVID-19, many governments decided to establish social distancing rules and stringent travel restrictions, including quarantines. Governments across Europe and the US have implemented financial assistance packages for companies. While a few industries, such as healthcare, are experiencing an increase in demand and are profiting from the crisis, most industries have been affected negatively. In fact, governmental restrictions caused the closure of restaurants and hotels, which resulted in very evident revenue reductions in the hospitality and tourism sector. It is already clear that state assistance, especially in Western countries, will be at levels far superior to those of all past crises.

2.3 The implications of the virus

The COVID-19 crisis has and will continue to have an enormous influence on businesses all over the world. From the moment the first case was reported in December 2019, new reports have appeared daily to explain the disastrous economic consequences that have hit the various economies around the world.[31] The most negative short-term effects landed largely on China because it was the starting point of the pandemic. Initially, China was the state that felt the negative effects more than any other state, while equally disastrous effects visited other states later. Several studies show how the COVID-19 outbreak caused previously unimaginable damage to the global supply chain because that supply chain relies heavily on Chinese manufacturing and raw materials.[32]

The rapid spread of COVID-19 meant that countries around the world had to adopt various public health measures and constraints to prevent and reduce the spread. One of these very widespread interventions has been social distancing.[33] As a consequence of social distancing, businesses, schools, community centres and Non-Governmental Organization (NGOs) had to close, mass gatherings were banned and lockdown measures were mandated in many countries, limiting travel to essential needs only. Social distancing aims to "flatten the curve", reducing the number of new daily cases linked to COVID-19 in order to stop explosive growth and reduce pressure on medical services.[34] Another important short-term consequence of the pandemic was the limited movement of people from one state to another. In some cases, the crossing of borders was prohibited, while in others, it was subject to very strict rules. Restrictions have also been placed within individual states and are not limited to people but also to commercial activities. In many cases, restrictions on the movement of people have also led to the immediate closure of commercial activities.

The travel industry has been affected most profoundly: airlines cut their workforce by 90%; 80% of hotel rooms have no guests. There was essentially no tourism in 2020. For example, in Italy, according to the Italian National Statistical Institute (ISTAT)[35] the reduction in tourist spending by Italians amounted to 50 billion euros. In addition, 207 million fewer foreigners visited Italy, and tourism's added value declined by 31.5%. The health crisis and the related measures to combat it led to a drastic drop in tourist flows in 2020, both in and out of our country. In terms of inbound tourism, 54.6% fewer foreigners visited Italy in 2020 than in 2019, with tourism spending topping out at 23.7 billion euros, a loss of about 35 billion euros compared to the previous year. In addition, sporting events, conferences, festivals and concerts were cancelled. Cultural venues, such as museums and galleries, also saw a drastic reduction in visits. Consulting in general, as well as personal services, like taxis, hairdressers and gyms, also experienced stagnation due to lockdowns.[36] Large electronics and automobile manufacturers suddenly closed (although they started to re-open two months after their closures).[37] The pandemic has led to demands to tighten production, as businesses close and people stay at home. Ultimately, the demand response during the pandemic has depended on the product type: essential or non-essential (including luxury).

There was the beginning of a slow recovery in 2021, but the recovery of losses remains a remote possibility. Since people have become worried about their safety, well-being and lives, they are saving money by avoiding unnecessary shopping and accumulating essential commodities (food and medicine). During the lockdown, people sought out essential goods, so the sale of those products increased, while the demand for luxury or non-essential products decreased significantly. Moreover, the supply and demand inconsistencies are resulting in a fall in employment opportunities, causing production cuts and business closures across economies. The International Labor Organization (ILO) warns that global unemployment could increase between 5.3 million (low-case scenario) and

24.7 million (high-case scenario) based on the estimate of global GDP growth, while the mid-case estimate forecasts an increase of about 13 million unemployed.[38] The ILO has also estimated that between 8.8 million (low-case scenario) and 35 million (high-case scenario) will fall into poverty worldwide (20.1 million average). Poor and developing countries will suffer the most, and for them, the job losses will be particularly important, as their economic activity depends on export-oriented industries.[39]

2.3.1 Macroeconomics implication

The effects of the COVID-19 outbreak are incredibly evident. Both lifestyles and social practices have been influenced by the consequences of the outbreak,[40] as well as the economic activities of people and firms.[41] In other words, everything from the micro and to the macro levels of people's lives has felt the influence of the pandemic.[42] In some countries, businesses have had to stop production and borders have been partially or completely closed. In China, for example, many large multinational companies had to temporarily suspend production. In addition, they temporarily halted the inbound and outbound air and sea transport routes.[43] The situation is especially unusual because the end of the pandemic remains uncertain and apparently in the fairly distant future. Therefore, many economic consequences will only be seen in the long term, as this situation of uncertainty leads to unpredictable reactions.[44]

According to Subourna (2020), it is possible to create a general map of the probable economic impacts of the COVID-19 pandemic, where the path is divided into five waves, highlighting what "could be" the duration of the impact and line of progress.[45] The first wave relates to the first phase, where the immediate and direct impact of the COVID-19 epidemic took the first countries by surprise. This led to the temporary closure of production and commercial activities. In the affected countries, there was a sharp and immediate decline in the economy. The second wave is the impact of internationalization. In addition to the worsening of the economy for internal reasons, the fact that the pandemic has spread all over the world has led to a substantial reduction in foreign demand. This has further aggravated internal economic situations by continuing to shrink production.[46] The third wave is the macroeconomic impact due to aggregate supply, demand and price level. The drop in demand has led to a reduction in production and supply, while disruptions in the supply chain cause chain-linked effects to the global supply chain. This is especially true when a country, like China, plays a key role in the global supply chain. The rest of the world, for instance, is significantly dependent on China for production inputs.[47] In addition, when domestic and international transport and logistics channels are suspended to stop the pandemic's spread, the supply chain is disrupted further. Therefore, a shock that simultaneously affects one country's production, demand, supply chain and even human flows will cause a significant reduction in international trade. If we see a reduction in supply and the simultaneous closure of transport routes in one country, the effect in the short term will be a reduction in the demand for imported goods and a smaller movement of people from one country to another. Exports and imports of both goods and services, including travel and tourism, will be significantly affected.[48] The reduction in the movement of people from one country to another combined with uncertainty and blocked transport and logistics causes an increase in costs and doubts about the future of the country's economy. International investors may be turned away, blocking their ongoing investment plans in the country.[49] Finally, the reduction of goods and services offered will lead to an increase in prices, which will tend to raise the price level of essential goods, as well as those that are usually imported.

The fourth wave effect is connected to the reduction of economic growth. If the key macro factors of an economy suffer shocks, the whole economy suffers. Economic growth, which is normally measured by the growth rate of gross domestic product (GDP), shows the consequences and impact. When an economy is adversely affected by the pandemic, it is faced with macro effects that will lead to a slowdown in GDP growth as a long-term effect.[50] If this effect continues over time and lasts through the third quarter of one year, the country's economy could enter a recession that can only be solved by economic activity that creates real GDP, real income, employment, industrial production and wholesale and retail sales.[51] The fifth wave is that of macro-relational impacts. The impact on economic growth could lead to a slowdown in growth or even a continuous decrease. This could also lead to a recession, possibly falling into an economic depression. It may be difficult to recover from a pandemic recession that could continue for an even longer period. All of this is compounded by the fact that institutions and politicians have no experience in managing a recession of this magnitude that is driven by a pandemic with no seeming end in sight.[52] It's possible that the COVID-19 pandemic will generate such a powerful loss of growth for many economies that millions will fall into poverty if no effective action is achieved.

2.3.2 Social implications

COVID-19 has resulted in tragic consequences for the economy, as well as for the health and lives of millions of people around the world.[53] During lockdowns, citizens have to stay at home, and even when they can go outside, it is necessary to respect the social distancing policies that[54] various states have adopted, which range widely from large-scale blockades to voluntary self-compliance measures.[55] Meanwhile, people are encouraged to stay home if they feel unwell and to limit social interaction whenever possible.[56] Moreover, school closures can have a negative impact on children and young people, in particular for students from low-income and single-parent families who struggle more with the closure of schools and childcare facilities along with a complete shift to digital education.[57] During the COVID-19 pandemic, digital courses and classes were difficult for underprivileged students to access, despite government efforts.

Another consequence of the lockdowns has been the radical rise in Internet and social media use. With the implementation of social distancing measures, working from home has increased. Thus, social media has become the main way to contact or socialize with others, and in many cases, the Internet is also the main way to get essential supplies and receive essential services.[58] On the one hand, isolation is useful for reducing infections; on the other hand, it causes loneliness and psychological problems. Researchers have also linked isolation with lower cognitive performance, depression and increased sensitivity.[59] This period is very difficult, not only for children but also for adults. Living at home 24/7 has caused an increase in domestic violence cases, quarrels between neighbours and arms sales.[60] However, social distancing has also resulted in an increase in other more constructive types of behaviour. For example, there has been an increase in purchases of cleaning products, more garbage is recycled, and people have started to develop new skills and take better care of their homes and the places they live.

2.3.3 Environmental and CSR implications

The COVID-19 pandemic represents one of the most significant ecological and environmental changes in recent history, which can have a potentially huge impact on the global environment and in particular on Corporate Social Responsibility (CSR).[61] The global lockdown and the slowdown of economic activities are expected to have a positive effect on the environment.[62] On the one hand, climate experts predict that greenhouse gas (GHG) emissions could decrease to proportions never seen before since World War II.[63] This outcome is mainly because of the social distancing measures adopted by governments following the emergence of the pandemic. China, the first country to have problems related to COVID-19, adopted important social distancing measures, and the main economic activities of the country were strongly affected. Industrial facilities arrested their production, and transportation significantly declined. All of this resulted in a dramatic reduction in the concentrations of nitrogen dioxide (NO_2) and particulate matter (PM) that have a diameter of less than 2.5 μm (PM 2.5) in the main Chinese cities.

In other parts of the world, the measures that were taken also led to a reduction in air contamination.[64] For example, in Europe, the governments of France, Germany, Italy and Spain required citizens to stay at home to contain the spread of the coronavirus. Therefore, the main production and commercial activities, as well as schools, were closed. Thus, the movement of people was reduced to a minimum, and the use of cars drastically decreased. All of this has led to a decrease in greenhouse gases (GHG).

Another positive aspect is that the social distancing measures adopted by numerous governments, which led to a reduction in tourism, also ensured that many beaches around the world are now cleaner than they have been in many years due to the reduction of waste that is normally produced by tourists visiting the beaches.[65]

Nevertheless, the COVID-19 pandemic has also had negative indirect effects on the environment. For example, in the US, some cities have ceased recycling programs because authorities have been concerned about the risk of diffusing the virus in recycling centres. Consumers' demand for online shopping and home delivery increased due to the quarantine rules established by the governments in many countries. Consequently, households generate a lot of organic waste, and since food purchased online is packed and shipped, inorganic waste has also increased. In Europe, companies that once encouraged (and sometimes required) consumers to bring their bags have increasingly moved to single-used packaging because sustainable waste management has been restricted. Italy, for example, prohibited ill residents from arranging their waste.

In terms of CSR implications, some people believe that the financial tensions caused by COVID-19 could lead firms to perform short-term gains but decrease long-term CSR investment due to lack of resources and pressure for survival.[66] Luckily, many companies have resisted dishonest business practices during this crisis and have actively participated in different CSR activities, such as those that helped fight the virus.[67] In the UK, as well as other countries, some manufacturing companies modified their production processes in order to adapt them for the production of fans, personal protective equipment, masks and hand sanitizers. Some produced these goods for the market, while others donated them. Vodafone, the telecommunications giant, has given free unlimited mobile data to many of their customers, focusing on the most vulnerable first.[68] Some companies donated commercial airtime to promote good causes, and banks focused on ethical initiatives, such as removing interest on overdrafts for a period of time and many others.[69]

Optimistically, the pandemic could lead to an acceleration of the development of (CSR). More and more companies and businesses are realizing that their long-term survival and development depend on achieving the delicate balance between attention to stakeholders and profitability. Therefore, this aspect could remain even after the pandemic and grow in the long term.[70] Although some companies may be ready to invest in CSR, they may still struggle with how to make these kinds of investments or how to invest effectively. The question that remains to be answered is: What is the best way to achieve beneficial and interdependent social, environmental and economic goals?

2.4 Suggestions for future pandemic outbreaks

The COVID-19 pandemic has been an extraordinary situational and contextual factor with considerable implications for both largely developed and small developing economies. Unfortunately, as of today, the end to this pandemic remains uncertain, and people worldwide are losing confidence due to this uncertainty.[71] Initially, treating the disease was the most urgent matter, overshadowing the impact on the economy. Economic problems, however, emerged quickly, so while implementing measures aimed at treating the disease is important, it is also always necessary to simultaneously plan and implement aggressive and innovative political actions with a long-term perspective to prevent economic crises.[72] Waiting until the end of the pandemic to take effective measures may be too late.

The consequences could be falling into an economic depression. Therefore, decisions and measures to combat the pandemic must go hand in hand with other measures, such as those to support the economy.

The main problem is that we are facing a new and totally different situation from any other economic crisis driven by known causes such as banking or financial crises. This is an unprecedented and unusual crisis.[73] Precisely because we are in a completely new situation, the traditional crisis management approach of thinking only of what is most urgent in the short term may not be the right answer. Measures taken should be comprehensive and not focus on a single activity or area of action; they should be "all inclusive" without neglecting some important areas. Furthermore, the measures must be designed with the long term, not just the short term, in mind, looking to the future to ensure that the desired effects are achieved. To tackle a global pandemic like the present one, which countries cannot deal with on their own, coordination at the supranational level is required.[74] We also need to pay close attention to the economies of poor and developing countries. These typically have a fragile economic environment with poor health infrastructure. It is important to help them during the pandemic and in the post-pandemic period to ensure that we all recover. The World Bank and other international institutions need to think about economic and health programs and packages specifically aimed at these countries.[75]

COVID-19 is not a one-off challenge, since it is likely that additional phases to the current pandemic or additional pandemics will occur in the future.[76] The best solution now is to be prepared for the next crisis (or the next phase of the current crisis) rather than responding reactively when the crisis strikes. Efforts should be made to grow from this valuable learning opportunity rather than taking a big sigh of relief and simply returning to normal routines. The COVID-19 crisis will modify businesses and society in important ways. For instance, it is likely to improve sectors such as online shopping, online education, and public health investments, and it is also likely to change how companies design their supply chains. It is important that companies consider the changes that the crisis induced in order to make their future plans sustainable. For instance, COVID-19 introduced organizational, administrative and medical challenges. Unfortunately, there is no information about how to manage a pandemic that produces this combination of difficulties; therefore, it is important to start thinking about strategies and procedures for alleviating uncertainty and handling a crisis to ease devastation and promote recovery.[77]

In doing so, it is essential that responsibility include various social partners to foster dialogue and stability.[78] All efforts must be combined in order to help people, workers and companies to overcome the crisis. The global economy needs urgent measures and policies that reach the real economy. Actions will have to be taken to keep workers in jobs, avoid unemployment, compensate for any loss of income and find other solutions to reduce the difficulties associated with the crisis, including financial difficulties. To build resilient companies, the following must be guaranteed: business continuity and income security. Security is key to ensuring the minimum means of subsistence and protecting people's lives.[79]

COVID-19 is a "wicked problem", which is a term used to identify concerns that are extremely difficult or even impossible to solve because they involve many interdependent, changing and difficult-to-define factors.[80] Addressing wicked problems requires systems thinking that recognizes the importance of unfamiliar internal operations (infection control, housekeeping, and materials management). In addition, it is important facing problems and analysing processes, establishing teams that focus internally and externally and can extend knowledge resourcing for developing ideas, and solving situations. Organizational support for workers that adopts learning rather than performance mindset and embraces the habit of quick implementation of iterative changes to respond to new problems that arise is critical for such creativity.[81] A learning mindset explores new ideas and practices, while a performance mindset follows and optimizes established practices. Learning mindsets, cultivated via organizational communications and practices, relieve unproductive performance pressure, freeing workers to offer and to experiment in order to develop effective solutions.[82]

COVID-19 requires teams that cross multiple functions and roles to provide coordinated responses in the midst of uncertainty. Effective teamwork depends on accurate, frequent, timely, and problem-solving communications reinforced by shared goals, shared knowledge and mutual respect, requirements collectively called relational coordination. Moreover, no organization can independently address the wicked problems presented by the scope and scale of COVID-19: this pandemic crosses demographic, geographic and organizational boundaries; therefore, forming and strengthening effective outside partnerships is key, whether with peer organizations, supply vendors, customer-patient groups or non-industry entities. Management research suggests that collaborative partnering is crucial to develop organizational and collective abilities to address wicked problems.[83]

Another important aspect is leadership, which is the process of engaging with others to set and achieve shared goals. This is indispensable in organizations, and even more so in times of crisis. Shared goals must be conveyed through clear, timely and transparent messages and actions. As previously mentioned, the COVID-19 pandemic offers great opportunities for companies who are actively engaged in sustainability and looking to adopt CSR principles. CSR will make it possible to improve and strengthen relationships with stakeholders by paying more attention to them. Consumers and communities are increasingly attentive to these issues, especially during the pandemic period. The bond of trust that is established between a company and its stakeholders becomes more significant and lasting during a pandemic than in "peaceful" times.[84]

All of these previously learnt lessons could help organizations, workers and patients to better manage the consequences of such disorder, uncertainty and change and provide the foundation for the emergence of that resilience, creativity and compassion that we need. As such, they provide a template for moving forward. Organizations implementing these actions can experience the benefits for themselves, their workers and their patients.

2.5 Importance of Resilience Management as a response to COVID-19

"Everything we do before a pandemic will seem alarmist, everything we do after a pandemic will seem inadequate" (US Health and Human Services Secretary Michael Leavitt in 2007).[85] The COVID-19 pandemic crisis, which has comparisons as a medical challenge, is an unprecedented situational and contextual event that is fundamentally different from any other in the past due to its social, economic and political context. Even the recent SARS-CoV crisis in 2002–2003 must be considered different because of COVID-19's incomparably higher contagion rate and the much larger number of goods and people traveling around the world now.[86] The lack of readiness in facing this global pandemic is evident among crisis managers and even eminent entrepreneurs, despite several warnings that were issued by medical experts. Many aspects of the crisis are strikingly similar to what has been widely discussed in risk management literature for decades, but the problem is that each crisis is different from the previous one and new crises of unforesee-able natures are likely to emerge in the future.[87]

Efficiency reigns in a stable world with no surprises and this mindset often dominates large corporations, but in a world characterized by future dynamic and unpredictable challenges, how is it possible to be prepared to face unforeseen or unknown shocks? How can we make the right, or at least good enough, societal choices once the threat has arrived?[88] There are fundamental ideologies and methodologies to rely upon.

According to conventional risk management, impossible risks should be mitigated before they cause severe problems. Nevertheless, we are living in a world that changes very rapidly and failures are inevitable, so such an option may be useless at safeguarding economies and social systems.[89] Therefore, the alternative approach is one that accepts the inherently unpredictable, uncertain and, at times, even random nature of the threats posed by the system and addresses them by building system resilience.[90] Resilience relies on the importance of system recovery and adaptation after disruption rather than trusting the ability of system operators to prevent, avoid and absorb all threats. Central systems need to be resilient. It's critical for them be able to adapt to ensure their survival into the future and even to take advantage of the new or revealed opportunities following the crisis to improve the system through broader systemic changes.[91] This is sometimes characterized as not just bouncing back to the pre-crisis conditions but designing policies and interventions to "bounce forward" towards a better and more sustainable pathway from economic, social and environmental points of view.[92]

COVID-19 is the latest instance of an unpredictable shock to interconnected systems, where international recovery will have important implications for future economic, social and governmental activity. Resilience should be an integral part of the philosophy for managing and operating the system in order to ensure the ability to continue to function even in the event of outages. Furthermore, the ability to adapt is important, so that we can identify how to improve later and know how to seize new or revealed opportunities.

The transboundary dynamics of COVID-19 present an unprecedented test of organizational resilience: resilience is not an outcome, but rather a process, by which organizations continuously work to anticipate and respond to external threats on a continuous basis. Where the unexpected happens, resilience involves the ability to continue functioning.[93] The strategic business model can be important where innovation, diversity, flexibility and the ability to work across boundaries may encourage new and adaptive approaches in the face of adversity.[94] In these circumstances, a resilient approach is crucial in order to be able "to face shocks and persistent structural changes in such a way that societal well-being is preserved and without compromising the heritage for future generations".[95]

When a system or a country is shocked, it is possible to activate different resilience capacities. When the time of exposure is not too long and the intensity is not too large, the most appropriate way to react might be through the absorptive capacity, which is the ability to value, assimilate, and apply new knowledge. As the time of exposure and its intensity increases, the adaptive capacity, namely the general ability of institutions, systems and individuals to adjust to potential damage, to take advantage of opportunities or to cope with the consequences, will start playing a role, strengthening flexibility and readiness for small changes.[96]

Ultimately, as disturbances become unbearable and adaptation would lead to too large a change, a transformation is needed to ensure that the system finds its new sustainable development path and avoids collapses. Resilient behaviour includes learning from past or current disturbances in order to improve resilience capacities or reduce subsequent risks. The COVID-19 shock is a major challenge and is so extreme in its duration and intensity that it is simply impossible to address it through absorptive capacities or a simple adaptation of the system; hence, the crisis should become an opportunity to progress and "bounce forward" through a combination of adaptation and transformation measures. Such a transformative resilience can strengthen the economic, social, environmental and institutional path and also mobilize the creativity of people and devotion needed to deal with the crisis.

Suitable adaptation and transformation should be incorporated to achieve long-term resilience after an environmental turbulence, in addition to mitigating the disturbance and bouncing back to previous states.[97] Previous states can be understood as organizations' original operational routines and decision-making patterns that have been frequently used for daily operations in static environments.

Thus, resilience can be viewed as an organization's active capacity to maintain its operational function and business performance before any structural changes (*absorptivity*), mitigate effects caused by crises (*adaptation*) and transform to a new state (*transformation*).

Resilience is also a dynamic and sustained state of organizational operations that requires various dynamic capabilities to continuously create new operational routines in a fast-changing operating environment.[98]

These capabilities are focused on the longer term and concerned with learning new approaches to cope with unexpected environmental turbulence. They enable organizations to build, renew and reconfigure resources in response to disruptions in the environment.[99] When organizations continuously encounter environmental turbulence (extreme weather and natural disasters), they need to develop adequate knowledge and skills to establish a set of new operational routines to cope with it.[100] Organizations, for example, should be able to make lasting changes inside their business model or structure to accelerate adaptation to unexpected events. In order for organizations to be resilient, they must be able to organize processes that enable them to learn from experience and use that knowledge to respond to future events.[101]

The modern world is characterized by the interconnections between systems, which are increasingly complex and dynamic. This is the result of economic opportunity and world-class interconnectedness and has brought major benefits to the majority of the global population.[102] One reaction to the COVID-19 outbreak could be to instinctively limit or reduce interconnections. However, it is not possible to stop the development of resilience in an international economic system. The evolution necessary for a post-COVID-19 world must take into account the resilience capacity, where systems must be designed to facilitate recovery and adaptation after a breakdown. Such recovery and adaptation are a requirement for the interconnected economic, industrial, social and health systems of our century, and resilience is an increasingly integrated and fundamental part of strategies for avoiding the collapse of the system itself.[103]

Resilient systems normally have common characteristics that should give responses to the crisis that is similar. The resilience literature provides recommendations aimed at building resilience to contain epidemics and other threats to the system.[104] To ensure functionality, access to additional manufacturing capacity and redundancies in system-crucial components can help smooth supply chain fluctuations; in the short term, companies may need to look beyond normal sources for solutions, but, in the longer term, redundancy can be built into the design. In normal times, having multiple approaches to compliance may be less efficient, but, at the same time, it is more flexible and resilient; therefore, it is more effective in crisis situations. The same is true for the diversity of ideas. This allows you to find different potential solutions and create a work team that is able to manage the crisis. Moreover, a corporate climate that is aimed at encouraging and respecting different ideas is also needed. Modular systems are another characteristic of resilient companies.[105] Modular systems, where factories, organizational units or sources of supply can be combined in different ways, ensure high resilience. In contrast, systems with a high degree of integration are very efficient but are not flexible; therefore, they are very vulnerable in cases of disturbance and can even collapse. Designing systems and developing methods for quantifying resilience so that the trade-off between a system's efficiency and resilience can be made explicit is the key to being resilient, recoverable and adaptable.

Assuring control of the system is important for minimizing failures resulting from unexpected events by breaking up needless connections between infrastructure and making required connections controllable and noticeable.[106] There are systems that are built to optimize and maximize efficiency and others that are designed to allow evolution and aimed at constantly improving their ability to seize opportunities, address problems or take into account new information. To give answers to dynamic crises such as COVID-19, systems are needed that prioritize evolution. Right and wrong answers become obsolete as situations change. Therefore, it is important to iterate and learn to find more effective solutions. Only after the fact will we know if many solutions were right or wrong, but this can help in the development of better future solutions. In the short term, this would appear to be the most effective strategy.[107]

The short-term strategy to be adopted should include developing tools to support decisions in real time, integrating data integration and automating the selection of management alternatives based on explicit political compromises in real time.[108]

Since the COVID-19 epidemic has arrived at a very high and uncertain infection point, another characteristic for the resilient organization is to be prudent by taking a fresh look at worst-case scenarios and develop contingency strategies. Another common trait is managing system topology by designing appropriate connections and communications across the interconnected infrastructure. Companies that do not carefully consider their stakeholders in the short term may seem to have an advantage because their management will be simpler; however, solutions that benefit a single company at the expense or neglect of others will create mistrust and do damage in the long term.[109] Conversely, customer support, partner support and attention to social systems in a time of adversity can potentially create lasting goodwill and commitment. Social dialogue is an essential element of building trust and confidence. Sharing relevant information is important to ensure that all parties concerned understand the nature of the impact of the COVID-19 crisis and know about any support measures that may be available to help alleviate problems and to demonstrate the need for change.

The uncertainty that characterizes our world along makes it very difficult to predict the next crisis and above all how it will be and where it will come from.

Even if one crisis is always different from another, learning from past events is always possible. Doing so can prevent the repetition of mistakes and lay the foundation for giving systemic responses to future crises.

Notes

1 Stöhr K., Esveld M., "Will vaccines be available for the next influenza pandemic?", *Science*, Vol. 306, 2004, pp. 2195–2196.
2 Naveen D., Gustafsson A., "Effects of COVID-19 on business and research", *Journal of Business Research*, Vol. 117, 2020, pp. 284–289; Qiu W., Rutherford S., Mao A., Chu C., "The pandemic and its impacts", *Health, Culture and Society*, Vol. 9, 2017, pp. 1–11.
3 Rewar S., Mirdha D., Rewar P., "Treatment and prevention of pandemic H1N1 influenza", *Annals of Global Health*, Vol. 81 No. 5, September–October 2015, pp. 645–653.
4 Maurice J., "Cost of protection against pandemics is small", *World Report*, Vol. 387 No. 10016, January 23, 2016, E12; WHO, *Ebola data and statistics, situation summary.* http://apps.who.int/gho/data/view. ebola-sitrep.ebola-summary-20160511?lang=en. Accessed September 21, 2017.
5 Jordà O., Singh S.R., Taylor A.M., "Longer-run economic consequences of pandemics", *The Review of Economics and Statistics*, 2021, pp. 1–29.
6 Donthu N., Gustafsson A., "Effects of COVID-19 on business and research", *Journal of Business Research*, Vol. 117, 2020, pp. 284–289.
7 Harris S.S., *A dictionary of epidemiology* (4th ed.). Oxford: Oxford University Press, 2000.
8 WHO, "The classical definition of a pandemic is not elusive", *Bulletin of the World Health Organization*, Vol. 89 No. 7, 2011, pp. 540–541.
9 Qiu W., Rutherford S., Mao A., Chu C., op. cit.
10 Taubenberger J.K., Morens D.M., "Pandemic influenza – Including a risk assessment of H5N1", *Revue Scientifique Et Technique-Office International Des Epizooties*, Vol. 28 No. 1, 2009, pp. 187–202.

11 Morens D.M., Folkers G.K., Fauci, A.S., "What is a pandemic?", *The Journal of Infectious Diseases*, Vol. 200 No. 7, 2009, pp. 1018–1021.

12 Morens D.M., Folkers G.K., Fauci, A.S., op. cit.

13 Qiu W., Rutherford S., Mao A., Chu C., "The pandemic and its impacts", *Health, Culture and Society*, Vol. 9, 2017, pp. 1–11.

14 Davies S.E., "National security and pandemics", *UN Chronicle*, Vol. 50, 2013, pp. 20–24.

15 Drake T.L., Chalabi Z., Coker R., "Cost-effectiveness analysis of pandemic influenza preparedness: What's missing?", *Bulletin of the World Health Organization*, Vol. 90 No. 12, 2012, pp. 940–941.

16 Nabarro D., Wannous C., "The links between public and ecosystem health in light of the recent ebola outbreaks and pandemic emergence", *EcoHealth*, 2016, pp. 1–3.

17 Cheema-Fox A., LaPerla B., Serafeim G., Hui W., Corporate resilience and response during COVID-19, Harvard Business School Working Paper, No. 20-108, April 2020.

18 Suborna B., Understanding coronanomics: The economic implications of the coronavirus (COVID-19) pandemic, MPRA Paper No. 99693, April 2020, pp. 1–45.

19 Kraus S., Clauss T., Breier M., Gast J., Zardini A., Tiberius, V., "The economics of COVID-19: Initial empirical evidence on how family firms in five European countries cope with the corona crisis", *International Journal of Entrepreneurial Behavior & Research*, Vol. 26 No. 5, 2020, pp. 1067–1092.

20 Huang X., et al., "Epidemiology and clinical characteristics of COVID-19", *Archives of Iranian Medicine*, Vol. 23 No. 4, April 2020, pp. 268–271; Chan J.F.-W. et al., "A familial cluster of pneumonia associated with the 2019 novel coronavirus indicating person-to-person transmission: A study of a family cluster", *Lancet* Vol. 395, 2020, pp. 514–523.

21 World Health Organization, Report of the WHO-China Joint Mission on Coronavirus Disease 2019 (COVID-19), 2020. Available online at: https://www.who.int/docs/default-source/coronaviruse/who-china-jointmission-on-covid-19-final-report.pdf

22 Cohen M.L., "Changing patterns of infectious disease", *Nature*, Vol. 406 No. 6797, 2000, pp. 762–767.

23 Suborna B., op. cit.

24 COVID Live – Coronavirus statistics – Worldometer. https://www.worldometers.info

25 Ourworldindata.org published by Statista.

26 Barua S., "Understanding coronanomics: The economic implications of the Covid-19 pandemic", *The Journal of Developing Areas*, Vol. 55 No. 3, 2021, pp. 435–450.

27 Baldwin R., di Mauro B., eds., *Economics in the time of COVID-19*. London: CEPR, 2020.

28 Kraus S., Clauß T., Breier M., Gast J., Zardini A., Tiberius V., "The economics of COVID-19: Initial empirical evidence on how family firms in five European countries cope with the corona crisis", *International Journal of Entrepreneurial Behavior & Research*, Vol. 26, April 2020, pp. 1067–1092.

29 Simchi-Levi D., Schmidt W., Wei, Y., "From superstorms to factory fires: managing unpredictable supply chain disruptions", *Harvard Business Review*, Vol. 92 No. 1–2, 2014, pp. 96–101.

30 del Rio-Chanona R.M., Mealy P., Pichler A., Lafond F., Farmer, D., "Supply and demand shocks in the COVID-19 pandemic: An industry and occupation perspective", *Oxford Review of Economic Policy*, 2020, graa033. arXiv preprint arXiv:2004.06759.

31 Brodeur A, Gray D, Islam A, Bhuiyan S., "A literature review of the economics of COVID-19", *Journal of Economic Surveys*, Vol. 35, 2021, pp. 1007–1044.

32 Sheffi Y., *The new (Ab) normal: Reshaping business and supply chain strategy beyond Covid-19*. Cambridge: MIT CTL Media, 2020; Sajjad, A., "The COVID-19 pandemic, social sustainability and global supply chain resilience: A review", *Corporate Governance*, Vol. 21 No. 6, 2021, pp. 1142–1154.

33 Fang Y.Q., Nie Y.T., Penny M., "Transmission dynamics of the COVID-19 outbreak and effectiveness of government interventions: A data-driven analysis", *Journal of Medical Virology*, Vol. 92 No. 6, 2020, pp. 645–659.

34 John Hopkins University, *New cases of COVID-19 in world countries*. Johns Hopkins Coronavirus Resource Center, 2020, Retrieved from https://coronavirus.jhu.edu/data/new-cases

35 ISTAT, Statistiche report, Conto satellite del turismo per l'Italia | anticipazione anno 2020, https://www.istat.it/it/files//2021/09/Conto-satellite-turismo-2020.pdf

36 He H, Harris L., "The impact of Covid-19 pandemic on corporate social responsibility and marketing philosophy", *Journal of Business Research*, Vol. 116, 2020, pp. 176–182.

37 Cheema-Fox A., LaPerla B., Serafeim G., Hui W., op. cit.

38 International Labor Organization, *ILO monitor: COVID-19 and the world of work* (8th ed.), Updated estimates and analysis, 2021.

39 Barua, S., Understanding Coronanomics: The economic implications of the coronavirus (COVID-19) pandemic, 2020. Available at SSRN 3566477.

40 Rožman M. Tominc P., "The physical, emotional and behavioral symptoms of health problems among employees before and during the COVID-19 epidemic", *Employee Relations*, ahead-of-print, 2021.

41 Golubeva O., "Firms' performance during the COVID-19 outbreak: international evidence from 13 countries", *Corporate Governance*, Vol. 21 No. 6, 2021, pp. 1011–1027.

42 Goel G., Dash S.R., "Investor sentiment and government policy interventions: Evidence from COVID-19 spread", *Journal of Financial Economic Policy*, ahead-of-print, 2021.

43 Zhang Y., Diao X., Chen K.Z., Robinson S., Fan S., "Impact of COVID-19 on China's macroeconomy and agri-food system – an economy-wide multiplier model analysis", *China Agricultural Economic Review*, Vol. 12 No. 3, 2020, pp. 387–407.

44 Ajmal M.M., Khan M., Shad, M.K., "The global economic cost of coronavirus pandemic: Current and future implications", *Public Administration and Policy: An Asia-Pacific Journal*, Vol. 24 No. 3, 2021, pp. 290–305.

45 Suborna B., op. cit.
46 Aljanabi A.R.A., "The impact of economic policy uncertainty, news framing and information overload on panic buying behavior in the time of COVID-19: A conceptual exploration", *International Journal of Emerging Markets*, ahead-of-print, 2021.
47 Osuna V., García Pérez J.I., "Temporary layoffs, short-time work and COVID-19: The case of a dual labour market", *Applied Economic Analysis*, ahead-of-print, 2021; Gunay S., Can G., Ocak M., "Forecast of China's economic growth during the COVID-19 pandemic: A MIDAS regression analysis", *Journal of Chinese Economic and Foreign Trade Studies*, Vol. 14 No. 1, 2021, pp. 3–17; Fracarolli Nunes M., Lee Park C., Paiva E., "Keeping key suppliers alive during the COVID-19 pandemic: artificial supply chain resilience and supplier crisis response strategies", *Continuity & Resilience Review*, Vol. 3 No. 3, 2021, pp. 282–299.
48 Anguera-Torrell O., Vives-Perez J., Aznar-Alarcón J.P., "Urban tourism performance index over the COVID-19 pandemic", *International Journal of Tourism Cities*, Vol. 7 No. 3, 2021, pp. 622–639; Shaikh I., Huynh T.L.D., "Does disease outbreak news impact equity, commodity and foreign exchange market? Investors' fear of the pandemic COVID-19", *Journal of Economic Studies*, ahead-of-print, 2021; Ajmal M.M., Khan M., Sha, M.K., AlKatheeri H., Jabeen F., "Empirical examination of societal, financial and technology-related challenges amid COVID-19 in service supply chains: Evidence from emerging market", *The International Journal of Logistics Management*, ahead-of-print, 2021.
49 Simon S., Sawandi N., Kumar S., El-Bannany M., "Economic downturns and working capital management practices: A qualitative enquiry", *Qualitative Research in Financial Markets*, Vol. 13 No. 4, 2021, pp. 529–554.
50 Suborna B., op. cit.
51 Claessens S., Ayhan Kose M., Terrones M.E., "What happens during recessions, crunches and busts?", *Economic Policy*, Vol. 24 No. 60, 1 October 2009, pp. 653–700.
52 Hassler J., "Macroeconomic perspectives on the corona crisis", in Fang, T. and Hassler, J. (Eds.), *Globalization, political economy, business and society in pandemic times (International Business and Management)*, Vol. 36. Bingley: Emerald Publishing Limited, 2021, pp. 41–50.
53 Donthu N., Gustafsson A., "Effects of COVID-19 on business and research", *Journal of Business Research*, Vol. 117, 2020, pp. 284–289.
54 Donthu N., Gustafsson A., op. cit.
55 Abel B., Gray D., Islam A., Bhuiyan S.J., A literature review of the economics of COVID-19, Institute of Labor Economics, Discussion Paper No. 13411, 2020.
56 Andersen M., Early evidence on social distancing in response to COVID-19 in the United States, April 5, 2020. Available at SSRN: https://ssrn.com/abstract=3569368 or http://dx.doi.org/10.2139/ssrn.3569368
57 Hynes W., Trump B., Love P., Linkov I., "Bouncing forward: A resilience approach to dealing with COVID-19 and future systemic shocks", *Environment Systems & Decision*, May 25, 2020, pp. 1–11.

58 Adekoya C.O., Fasae J.K., "Social media and the spread of COVID-19 infodemic", *Global Knowledge, Memory and Communication*, ahead-of-print, 2021; Riaz M., Wang X.S., Guo Y., "An empirical investigation of precursors influencing social media health information behaviors and personal healthcare habits during coronavirus (COVID-19) pandemic", *Information Discovery and Delivery*, Vol. 49 No. 3, 2021, pp. 225–239.

59 Pronzato R., Risi E., "Reframing everyday life. Implications of social distancing in Italy", *International Journal of Sociology and Social Policy*, ahead-of-print, 2021.

60 Campbell A.M., "An increasing risk of family violence during the Covid-19 pandemic: Strengthening community collaborations to save lives", *Forensic Science International: Reports*, 2020.

61 He H., Harris L., "The impact of Covid-19 pandemic on corporate social responsibility and marketing philosophy", *Journal of Business Research*, Vol. 116, May 2020; Carroll A.B., "Corporate social responsibility (CSR) and the COVID-19 pandemic: Organizational and managerial implications", *Journal of Strategy and Management*, Vol. 14 No. 3, 2021, pp. 315–330.

62 Almond R.E.A., Grooten M., Petersen T., eds. *WF (2020) Living Planet Report 2020 – Bending the curve of biodiversity loss*. Gland, Switzerland: WWF, 2020.

63 Global Carbon Project, Global Carbon Budget, 2021.

64 Borojo D.G., Yushi J., Miao, M., "The effects of COVID-19 on trade, production, environmental quality and its implications for green economy", *Journal of Economic Studies*, ahead-of-print, 2021.

65 Zambrano-Monserrate M.A., Ruano M.A., Sanchez-Alcalde L., "Indirect effects of COVID-19 on the environment", *Science of the Total Environment*, Vol. 728, 2020, p. 138813.

66 Ahmed J.U., Islam Q.T., Ahmed A., Faroque A.R., Uddin, M.J., "Corporate social responsibility in the wake of COVID-19: multiple cases of social responsibility as an organizational value", *Society and Business Review*, Vol. 16 No. 4, 2021, pp. 496–516.

67 Awawdeh A.E., Ananzeh M., El-khateeb A.I., Aljumah A., "Role of green financing and corporate social responsibility (CSR) in technological innovation and corporate environmental performance: A COVID-19 perspective", *China Finance Review International*, ahead-of-print, 2021.

68 BBC, "Coronavirus: Vodafone offers 30 days free mobile data", *The BBC*, accessible at: https://www.bbc.co.uk/news/technology-52066048, accessed 18 April 2020; BBC, "Alibaba's Ma donates coronavirus test kits to US", *The BBC*, accessible at: https://www.bbc.co.uk/news/business-51904379, accessed 18 April, 2020; BBC, "Coronavirus: Twitter boss pledges $1bn for relief effort", *The BBC*, accessible at: https://www.bbc.co.uk/news/technology-52209690, accessed 18 April, 2020.

69 He H., Harris L., "The impact of Covid-19 pandemic on corporate social responsibility and marketing philosophy", *Journal of Business Research*, Vol. 116, 2020, pp. 176–182.

70 Grunwald G., Schwill J., Sassenberg A.M., "Sustainability project partnerships in times of crisis: conceptual framework and implications for stakeholder integration", *Journal of Entrepreneurship and Public Policy*, Vol. 10 No. 3, 2021, pp. 352–378.

71 Suborna B., op. cit.; Villi B., "The influence of Covid-19 on consumers' perceptions of uncertainty and risk", in Grima S., Özen E., Boz H. (Eds.), *Contemporary issues in social science (contemporary studies in economic and financial analysis*, Vol. 106. Bingley: Emerald Publishing Limited, 2021, pp. 135–148.

72 Aljanabi A.R.A., "The impact of economic policy uncertainty, news framing and information overload on panic buying behavior in the time of COVID-19: A conceptual exploration", *International Journal of Emerging Markets*, ahead-of-print, 2021.

73 Čadil J., Beránek M., Kovář V., "Likely winners and losers in upcoming COVID-19 economic crisis—Lessons learned from the GFC", *Journal of Entrepreneurship in Emerging Economies*, Vol. 13 No. 4, 2021, pp. 575–587.

74 Joyce S. Osland, J. S., Mark E. Mendenhall, M. E., Reiche, B. S., Szkudlarek, B., Bolden, R., Courtice, P., Vaiman, V., Vaiman, M., Lyndgaard, D., Nielsen, K., Terrell, S., Taylor, S., Lee, Y., Stahl, G., Boyacigiller, N., Huesing, T., Miska, C., Zilinskaite, M., Ruiz, L., Shi, H., Bird, A., Soutphommasane, T., Girola, A., Pless, N., Maak, T., Neeley, T., Levy, O., Adler, N., Maznevski, M., "Perspectives on global leadership and the COVID-19 crisis", in Osland J.S., Szkudlarek B., Mendenhall M.E., Reiche B.S. (Eds.), *Advances in global leadership (advances in global leadership)*, Vol. 13. Bingley: Emerald Publishing Limited, 2020, pp. 3–56.

75 Goel G., Dash S.R., "Investor sentiment and government policy interventions: Evidence from COVID-19 spread", *Journal of Financial Economic Policy*, ahead-of-print, 2021.

76 Reeves M., Lang N., Carlsson-Szlezak P., "Lead your business through the coronavirus crisis", *Harvard Business Review Digital Article*, H05GBP-PDF-ENG, 2020.

77 Nembhard I.M., Burns Lawton R., Shortell S., "Responding to Covid-19: Lessons from management research", *NEJM Catalyst Innovations in Care Delivery*, 2020.

78 International Labour Organization (ILO), Joint statement on COVID-19 by international organization of employers and international trade union confederation, Geneva, 2020.

79 Purnomo B.R., Adiguna R., Widodo W., Suyatna H., Nusantoro B.P., "Entrepreneurial resilience during the Covid-19 pandemic: Navigating survival, continuity and growth", *Journal of Entrepreneurship in Emerging Economies*, Vol. 13 No. 4, 2021, pp. 497–524.

80 Johnstone I., "The G20, climate change and COVID-19: Critical juncture or critical wound?", *Fulbright Review of Economics and Policy*, Vol. 1 No. 2, 2021, pp. 227–245.

81 Dayrit M.M., Mendoza R.U., "Social cohesion vs COVID-19", *International Journal of Health Governance*, Vol. 25 No. 3, 2020, pp. 191–203.

82 Slagle D., McIntyre J.J., Chatham-Carpenter A., Reed H.A., "The perfect storm in the midst of a pandemic: The use of information within an institution's concurrent crises", *Online Information Review*, Vol. 45 No. 4, 2021, pp. 656–671.

83 Arslan A., Golgeci I., Khan Z., Al-Tabbaa O., Hurmelinna-Laukkanen P., "Adaptive learning in cross-sector collaboration during global emergency: Conceptual insights in the context of COVID-19 pandemic", *Multinational Business Review*, Vol. 29 No. 1, 2021, pp. 21–42.

84 He H., Harris L., op. cit.

85 Hynes W., Trump B., Love P., Linkov I., "Bouncing forward: A resilience approach to dealing with COVID-19 and future systemic shocks", *Environment Systems & Decisions*, 2020 May 25, pp. 1–11.

86 Zhang R., et al., "Identifying airborne transmission as the dominant route for the spread of COVID-19", *Proceedings of the National Academy of Sciences of USA*, Vol. 117 No. 6, October 2020.

87 Giovannini E., Benczur P., Campolongo F., Cariboni J., Manca A., *Time for transformative resilience: The COVID-19 emergency*, EUR 30179 EN. Luxembourg: Publications Office of the European Union, 2020.

88 Reeves M., Lang N., Carlsson-Szlezak P., "Lead your business through the coronavirus crisis", *Harvard Business Review Digital Article*, H05GBP-PDF-ENG, 2020.

89 Michel-Kerjan E., "How resilient is your country?", *Nature News*, Vol. 491 No. 7425, 2012, p. 497; Linkov I., Trump B.D., *The science and practice of resilience*, Berlin: Springer, 2019.

90 Mokline B., Ben Abdallah M.A., "Organizational resilience as response to a crisis: Case of COVID-19 crisis", *Continuity & Resilience Review*, Vol. 3 No. 3, 2021, pp. 232–247; Remko V.H., "Research opportunities for a more resilient post-COVID-19 supply chain – Closing the gap between research findings and industry practice", *International Journal of Operations & Production Management*, Vol. 40 No. 4, 2020, pp. 341–355.

91 Hynes W., Trump B., Love P., Linkov I., "Bouncing forward: A resilience approach to dealing with COVID-19 and future systemic shocks", *Environment Systems and Decisions*, Vol. 40, 2020, pp. 174–184.

92 Bryce C., Ring P., Ashby S., Wardman J. K., "Resilience in the face of uncertainty: Early lessons from the COVID-19 pandemic", *Journal of Risk Research*, Vol. 23, 2020, pp. 880–887.

93 Wildavsky A.B., *Searching for safety*. Piscataway, NJ: Transaction Publishers, 1988; Weick K.E., Sutcliffe K.M., *Managing the unexpected: Resilient performance in an age of uncertainty*. San Francisco, CA: Jossey-Bass, 2007.

94 Meyer A.D., "Adapting to environmental jolts", *Administrative Science Quarterly*, Vol. 27 No. 4, 1982, pp. 515–537; Hamel G., Valikangas L., "The quest for resilience", *Harvard Business Review*, Vol. 81 No. 9, 2003, pp. 52–65.

95 Giovannini E., Benczur P., Campolongo F., Cariboni J., Manca A., *Time for transformative resilience: The COVID-19 emergency*, EUR

30179 EN. Luxembourg: Publications Office of the European Union, 2020.

96 Giovannini E., Benczur P., Campolongo F., Cariboni J., Manca A., op. cit.

97 Jiang Y., Ritchie B.W., Verreynne M L., "Building tourism organizational resilience to crises and disasters: A dynamic capabilities view", *International Journal of Tourism Research*, Vol. 21 No. 6, 2019, pp. 882–890.

98 Gibson C.A., Tarrant M A., "A 'conceptual models' approach to organisational resilience", *Australian Journal of Emergency Management*, Vol. 25 No. 2, 2010, pp. 6–12.

99 Pisano G.P., Teece D.J., "How to capture value from innovation: Shaping intellectual property and industry architecture", *California Management Review*, Vol. 50 No. 1, 2007, pp. 278–296.

100 Jiang Y., Ritchie B.W., Verreynne M L., op. cit.

101 Berkes F., "Understanding uncertainty and reducing vulnerability: Lessons from resilience thinking", *Natural Hazards*, Vol. 41 No. 2, 2007, pp. 283–295.

102 Hynes W., Trump B., Love P., Linkov I., op. cit.

103 Merad M., Trump B., *Expertise under scrutiny*. New York: Springer International Publishing, 2020.

104 Reeves M., Lang N., Carlsson-Szlezak P., "Lead your business through the coronavirus crisis", *Harvard Business Review Digital Article*, H05GBP-PDF-ENG, 2020.

105 Adobor H., "Supply chain resilience: An adaptive cycle approach", *The International Journal of Logistics Management*, Vol. 31 No. 3, 2020, pp. 443–463.

106 Polyviou M., Croxton K.L., Knemeyer A.M., "Resilience of medium-sized firms to supply chain disruptions: The role of internal social capital", *International Journal of Operations & Production Management*, Vol. 40 No. 1, 2020, pp. 68–91.

107 Reeves M., Lang N., Carlsson-Szlezak P., "Lead your business through the coronavirus crisis", *Harvard Business Review*, Vol. 27, 2020, pp. 2–7.

108 Modgil S., Singh R.K., Hannibal C., "Artificial intelligence for supply chain resilience: Learning from Covid-19", *The International Journal of Logistics Management*, ahead-of-print, 2021.

109 Datta P., "Supply network resilience: A systematic literature review and future research", *The International Journal of Logistics Management*, Vol. 28 No. 4, 2017, pp. 1387–1424.

3 The Impact of COVID-19 on the Italian Tourism Sector

3.1 The importance of tourism and its dimensions

According to the World Travel & Tourism Council (WTTC), the travel & tourism sector experienced a loss of almost US$4.7 trillion in 2020, with the contribution to GDP decreasing by an astonishing 49.1% compared to 2019, relative to a 3.7% GDP decrease of the global economy in 2020.[1] In 2019, the sector contributed 10.4% to global GDP, a share which decreased to 5.5% in 2020 due to continuing mobility restrictions. Moreover, 62 million jobs were lost in 2020, representing a decrease of 18.5%, leaving just 272 million employed across the tourism sector globally, compared to 334 million in 2019. The United Nations World Tourism Organization's (UNWTO) World Tourism Barometer highlighted that international tourists (overnight visitors) in the period from July-September 2021 increased by 58% compared to the same period in 2020. However, that is still 64% fewer international tourists during the same period in 2019. Internationally, Europe is positioned slightly better in the third quarter, with international arrivals declining by 53% compared to the same quarter of 2019.[2]

Tourism is a central aspect of modern society, and it affects every component of the world and every person in the world. Tourism's core is the physical movement of people: ever since the beginning of the human race, people have travelled for various reasons. The main reason for travelling during ancient times was war and the territorial expansion of countries through conquering.[3] Throughout the Middle Ages, with the discovery and exploration of America and later Australasia, this process continued, although during these times, religion was a major motivator of travel, as the devoted departed for pilgrimages. Until the 1840s, tourism remained a pursuit of the rich, who were able to travel for months at a time, exploring Europe and the edges of Africa and Asia to learn about cultures

DOI: 10.4324/9781003268963-4

and bring back new ideas for architecture and society. After the aristocracy had led the way, the rest of society was able to follow. The advance of steam railways, the advent of paid holidays and the emergence of seaside resorts resulted in the working classes travelling in masses.[4]

The development of the tourism phenomenon can be divided into four different phases.[5] The first stage of tourism is called "proto tourism" or "origins tourism" and covers a period of over 1,000 years, from ancient times to the industrial revolution. It refers to an elite tourism that involved the nobility, the aristocracy and the religious and had its origins in the Grand Tour, which was a training trip to major cities and areas of European artistic and cultural interest. Travel was not motivated by pleasure, and the flows were very small. The second evolutionary stage of tourism is "modern tourism", which developed over the years between the industrial revolution and the decennium 1930–1940. Tourist flows significantly increased at this time thanks to advancements in transportation networks and the inauguration of paid holidays for workers, which enabled the democratization of tourism. This process extended the opportunity to travel beyond the restricted circle of aristocratic social classes and to the middle classes. During this phase, the first responsive and receptive structures, as well as new professions related to tourism, were developed.

The advent of industrial growth and the consequent economic rise allowed the affirmation of tourism in mass, characteristic of the period from the second postwar to the early years of the neo-industrial era. The new element is represented by the presence among tourists of all classes social. Most of the tourist flows are concentrated in certain destinations and this favours the standardization of demand and supply. The accommodation facilities in the area increase and begin to organize themselves through one managerial management. The first travel agencies and the first tour operators are established. The last evolutionary stage that characterized the years from 1990 onwards is that of tourism global. The tourist is now an independent subject, who seeks an authentic contact with the local reality; he is more and more informed and more and more demanding, therefore he hires greater emphasis on the motivation of the trip, as well as the search for new adventures and emotions. The specialized accommodation facilities are completely oriented towards marketing and therefore able to offer diversified services and propose offers to the customer tourism ad hoc to satisfy their needs and expectations.[6]

What has happened in the last 20–30 years is an increased refining in the travel consumer, and the growing body of tourism research is evidencing that the act of travel and the role of a tourist is complex and heavy of sociological discourses around the reasons why people travel, what they seek and how they remember a tourist space.[7] It is a consequence of increased awareness, better education and increased competition in the marketplace, and a better understanding of customer requirements, combined with improved media and technology that have led to more specialized tourism activities.[8]

3.2 Typologies of tourism

There are two main typologies of travellers: those who travel for work and those who travel for personal reasons—for example, to visit family or friends, to study, to engage in a religious pilgrimage or experience, for their health, to play or watch sports, and many more.[9] For the first type of traveller, the decisions about their travel, including where to go, are largely outside their control. Business travellers have less discretion in their choice of destination or length of stay since business trips are usually organized without much advance, with a specific purpose and for a short period of time. In business travel, the goal is not to visit locations and enjoy their attractions and facilities. Instead, business travellers need the convenience of frequent, regular transportation facilities, trustworthy services and good housing.[10] Moreover, working travellers are often less worried about the cost of travel since their employer is paying for the arrangements. Leisure travellers, on the other hand, are considerably attentive to cost, especially those travellers who are price sensitive. Destinations with lower prices are attractive to a larger number of travellers. Tourists who are sensitive about expenses usually make their holiday plans according to the costs. They are often willing to travel on days that cost less and to book well in advance of their travel dates if this allows them to have lower travel prices.[11]

Tourism has also been categorized based on the movement of people, as well as more detailed travel purposes.[12] In terms of the first classification, tourism can be classified as national or international. International tourism is when people visit a country that is foreign to their country of residence. International tourism can be inbound or outbound. Inbound tourism refers to tourists of external origin entering another country. When tourists travel from their country of origin to another country, they represent outbound tourism for their country of origin because they are travelling outside their own country.

Another type of classification distinguishes tourism into six distinct categories according to the traveller's purpose and destination: pleasure and recreational tourism, business tourism, sports tourism, health and medical tourism, cultural tourism and religious tourism.[13] Pleasure and recreational tourism include tourism for improving one's physical or spiritual well-being, recovering from the fatigue and exhaustion of work, getting some fresh air, fulfilling one's curiosity, relaxing one's muscles, looking at something new, enjoying the beautiful scenery, and more. This type of tourism can be done at destinations like seaside getaways, mountains, health centres, rehabilitation centres and resorts.[14] In support of recreational activities, the Italian government has taken on an important role in creating, maintaining and organizing recreational spaces, and whole industries have developed merchandise or services.[15] This category includes nature tourism, where the main objective is to experience and enjoy nature, such as farms and wildlife. Natural tourism also includes rural tourism and ecotourism.[16] Ecotourism is a form of responsible tourism in natural areas that focuses on the conservation of the environment, including flora and fauna. Ecotourism also aims to improve the well-being of the local population, who can benefit from the low-impact activities and a limited number of visitors that characterize ecotourism—unlike mass tourism, which is more commercial and based on large numbers.[17] Rural tourism includes tourism related to lakes and mountain tourism. Broadly, it can also be seen as including excursions in the countryside, food and wine trips, farm holidays, visits and stays in rural retreats, river holidays, visits to wildlife parks and national parks, etc.[18]

Business tourism is for conducting business transactions and attending business meetings, workshops, conferences, etc. The objective of business tourism is mainly professional and related to one's job.[19]

Sports/adventure tourism is divided into big sports events like the Olympic Games and various World Championships that attract visitors or fans and the tourism of practitioners, who want to engage in sporting activities like mountain climbing, horseback riding, hunting, fishing, etc. Health and medical tourism involve people travelling for medical treatment or visiting spas or resorts that offer curative possibilities.[20] In the past, this term may have referred to those who travelled from less-developed countries to major medical centres situated in highly developed countries (typically, for treatments that were unavailable in the tourists' home country). Cultural tourism aims at increasing one's understanding of a place, including local history, productions and culture.[21] This type of tourism satisfies cultural and intellectual curiosity and often includes studying at a research centre, visiting historical monuments or museums, or participating in local festivals for the arts, theatre, folk dance, etc. Religious tourism is not always and only linked to traditional religious practices, such as pilgrimage; it can also be for meditation or even for leisure. Some travel alone, while others prefer a group.[22] The success of the tourism industry is largely the result of the positive links that exist across different tourism-related service sectors. The combination of all services is what transforms a trip into an experience.[23]

3.3 The sectors of tourism

Basically, four main sectors — transportation, accommodation, ancillary services and sales and distribution — comprise the tourism industry.

3.3.1 Transportation

The possibility for tourists to move comfortably and quickly from one place to another is what enabled the development of tourism. Without modern transportation, tourism would not have its contemporary dimensions. Tourists can travel by land, air and water. The chosen mode of transportation often depends on the distance one is travelling. Air travel is mainly used when the destinations to be reached are far away. Car and train are preferred for shorter distances. Different means of transport are usually used within host destinations. Tourists often enjoy experimenting with different forms of transportation, which can add colour to their overall tourism experience. Many countries offer unusual forms of transportation, including cable cars, funicular railways, monorail, punting, jetboating and rafting, among other options. There are also many forms of water transportation, including ocean cruises, ferries and hovercrafts, passenger cargo ships, river cruises, house boats and yacht charters.

3.3.2 Accommodation

The accommodation sector comprises different forms of hospitality facilities that can be conveniently categorized as service (where catering is included) or self-catering establishments. Service accommodations consist of hotels, bed and breakfasts (B&B's), hostels and other similar establishments. Self-catering accommodations may include campsites, caravans, holiday room rentals, villas, apartments, chalets, etc. Hotels are the most used overnight accommodation services. The hotel's location is usually the most critical factor affecting its profitability. In addition to the location, the price, services offered and reviews from other tourists are important for the success of any tourist accommodation.[24]

Large, multinational hotel chains developed as a popular mode of accommodation for mass tourism. This type of accommodation is also based on franchising. Often, these hotels and motels belong to large chains but are run by individual franchisees who pay royalties to their parent companies for the privilege of operating under their brand and for other services. The advantage of belonging to these large chains is benefiting from their websites and other forms of advertising and communication. Their advertisements are often very aggressive and widespread in order to reach the highest possible number of potential customers. They use different channels for different types of customers; for example, they have agreements with tour operators to facilitate contact with customers who do not like technology.

For people who prefer to get closer contact with local people and culture, the suitable forms of accommodation are a Bed and Breakfast (B&B) or a guesthouse.[25] These are forms of accommodation that are normally family run and can cater to all types of travellers, both leisure and business. B&Bs appeal to travellers who prefer informality and friendliness to crowded, formal hotels. Farmhouses are also a kind of accommodation for those who do not like crowded hotels. These are especially widespread in villages with a strong agricultural tradition, such as, for example, in European countries.[26] Agritourism has also become popular as the behaviours and tastes of travellers have changed. Now, many people prefer a healthy lifestyle, including the consumption of natural foods and staying outdoors. Various public and private entities have provided money to help farmers transform their farms into tourist accommodation facilities.[27]

Some tourists, for reasons of convenience and safety, prefer to have a second home, either owned or with a long-term rental, which can be used for seasonal, recreational or occasional use. There are also timeshares, which are a kind of "vacation ownership" that allows multiple owners to use the same accommodation. Each user has the right to use the property for a fixed period of time, which is usually one week per year. Other tourist accommodations include those related to education. For example, many university colleges rent rooms, which are normally intended for students, during the summer months when students are not present. The sharing economy has also ushered in a new type of accommodation: shared accommodation. Normally, it's peer-to-peer sharing that uses an online marketplace.[28] The sharing economy is based on using technology to match those who have an excess of resources with those who need them and to enable each party to share their necessary information quickly and easily.[29] A good example is Airbnb, an online marketplace that allows people to lease or rent their accommodation. Airbnb is not the owner of the accommodations; it is only an intermediary and is remunerated with the commissions of both the guests and the hosts, for each booking. Through the web platform, it is possible to book entire houses or private or shared rooms. The website is very simple, and users can use different filters, such as price, available services and type of accommodation, to facilitate their search.[30] Usually, shared accommodation is cheaper than hotels, especially in urban areas.

3.3.3 Ancillary Services

Tourists on holiday like to be amused, entertained and active. Thus, they require information about their destination's ancillary services, including activities and attractions, such as shopping, catering, Wi-Fi and business centre access, infrastructure, interpreters, financial services, tourist guides, entertainment and more.

3.3.4 Sales and distribution

In addition to the main sectors, it is important to analyse the provision of support services related to tourism. There are various service providers involved in the sale of these services, such as airlines, hotels, transport companies, tour operators and travel agencies. How services are purchased has changed over time, and today consumers prefer to make purchases through digital systems. Therefore, many service providers and tour operators sell directly from their corporate websites or through travel search engines (where online visitors can compare prices).

3.4 New forms of tourism

After playing a critical role in the history of many countries, tourism has gradually obtained an autonomous space in the economy, in law and in the organization of social services. The dimensions reached by tourist traffic have helped to transform tourism from a sector linked to the production economy to one linked to the consumer economy.[31] This new approach has, in fact, entailed an expansion of the connotative sphere, which includes political and social aspects, acquiring a highly significant value in the collective individual life. This constantly evolving sector is not only changing the tourist offer models but is also witnessing a real change in market demand. In fact, tourism companies must be able to overcome important challenges to achieve success by responding through innovation, the use of technology, different and new marketing programs, and qualified and experienced staff, acquiring ever closer ties with their customers with the goal of being able to anticipate their needs and guarantee customer satisfaction. In particular, today, the centrality and attention must be directed not so much towards how travellers, but towards how they live and what they look for in a holiday experience.

Travellers increasingly appreciate the use of technology and are increasingly sophisticated in their search, selection and purchase of accommodations away from the big chains. Tourists have become creative and are looking for new opportunities to make their holidays unique and to have personalized experiences away from mass tourism.[32] A change in the tourist profile is, therefore, evident. Rather than being a spectator, as in the past, tourists now want to be the protagonist of their trip by actively participating in it and sharing their experience with other people. This change has led to the past concept of a holiday as an escape from the habits and regularities of daily life being put aside in favour of a vision of the tourist experience as a deepening and widening of people's habitual experiential world.

Globalization, as well as the evolution of consumption, has contributed to the decline of mass tourism and the rise of alternative forms of tourism. Alternative tourism is understood as the set of forms of tourism consistent with natural, social and community values that allow all stakeholders to enjoy both positive and valid interactions and shared experiences.[33] The presence of ethical values, such as reducing one's environmental impact and respecting and protecting the environments and traditional cultures of local populations, as well as the active participation of locals in the management of tourism businesses, are some of the elements common to new forms of tourism.[34] These emerging forms of tourism share four features[35]:

1 Landscape: attention to the natural and landscape dimension of the destination.
2 Leisure: leisure as a form of entertainment.
3 Learning: learning and discovering the traditions, history and culture of the destination in all its expressions.
4 Limit: the awareness and acceptance of limiting the use of places to ensure and preserve their resources in the medium to long term.

The World Tourism Organization (UNWTO) defined sustainable tourism in 1988[36]:

> Tourist activities are sustainable when they develop in such a way as to remain viable in a tourist area for an unlimited time, they do not alter the environment (natural, social and artistic) and do not hinder or inhibit the development of other social and economic activities.[37]

The concept refers to the more general definition of sustainable development given by the World Commission on Environment and Development in the Brundtland Report in 1987. The link between sustainable tourism and local communities has also been emphasized in numerous institutional documents and communications, among which is the "Lanzarote Charter for Sustainable Tourism" of 1995. This document states that tourism development must be based on the criterion of long-term sustainability; that is, the tourist offer must be economically convenient and ethically and socially fair with regard to local communities. The same Charter establishes three key rules on which the development of sustainable tourism must be based: (1) environmental resources must be protected and guaranteed; (2) local communities must benefit from this type of tourism, both in terms of income and quality of life; and (3) tourists must have an integrated experience with the host community.

There are several reasons that explain the development of sustainable tourism.[38] First, there are purely psychological and emotional reasons: restlessness and boredom are part of the search for great personal experiences. Tourists yearn for places and experiences that they can define as the perfect holiday. This desire, in general, is not satisfied by mass, standardized holidays, but seeks different, new, less-explored paths, capable of transmitting value and well-being. From this point of view, some studies consider sustainable tourism as the natural reaction to the impact of mass tourism. Contrary to mass tourism, sustainable tourists want to be able to personalize their holiday, moving freely through different types or levels of activity, from sports to environmental, from food and wine to culture, etc., thus placing themselves as an experimental subject, open to human and naturalistic experiences. More recently, this type of tourist has also become more flexible, ecological and attentive to the quality of the products they consume, all as an expression of a society that is more aware of the problems of sustainability and social responsibility. Some of the new forms of tourism that share an interest in sustainability are ecotourism, responsible tourism, slow tourism and proximity tourism.

Ecotourism is characterized as a type of tourism aimed at favouring the natural, social and artistic environment of a destination, trying not to hinder the development of other social and economic activities typical of the area. Ecotourism refers to forms of tourism that are based in nature and in which tourists' main motivation of the appreciation of nature itself as well as traditional cultures. Ecotourism generally contains educational and interpretative features and is organized by specialized tour operators for small groups. Moreover, the destination service providers tend to be small local businesses, minimize negative impacts on the natural and socio-cultural environment, and support the protection of natural areas.[39] Ecotourism addresses social and environmental objectives by conserving biodiversity, supporting wildlife and protected areas, diversifying livelihoods, and strengthening institutions of resource management.[40] Finally, ecotourism is an activity specifically designed with the aim of channelling visitor revenues to conservation activities and improving the well-being of the local population.

Responsible tourism is based on principles of social and economic justice and respect for the environment and cultures. Responsible tourists recognize the centrality of the host community and its right to be a protagonist in sustainable tourism development. Moreover, it favours the positive interaction between all the subjects involved. Responsible tourism arises from the need to protect local communities and to involve indigenous populations, who have been victims of problems related to mass tourism. The concept of responsibility extends to various forms of tourism, such as solidarity, fair and community tourism, and becomes a theoretical reference regardless of the destination.[41] The subjects involved in this tourist practice are aware of themselves and their actions. They are respectful towards the stakeholders and the places they visited. They want to learn about new cultures and support their host communities.

Slow tourism is a way of travelling that arises in response to the frenzy of everyday life. It is a form of tourism that respects local cultures, history and the environment. Furthermore, it values social responsibility by highlighting diversity and connecting people.[42] Slow tourism promotes a culture of hospitality, with particular respect for the environment and protection of cultural, artistic and monumental heritages.[43] Slowness represents a different way of managing time in order to meet local communities, learn about their traditions, customs and habits and live every moment of the journey with intensity. Slow tourism includes various transportation practices, such as cycling and trekking. Cycle tourism is a form of sustainable tourism that allows visitors to experience an area in which the environmental and social dimensions of life are preserved. It also enhances the issues of land protection and is a strategic asset for environmental socio-cultural protection and for economic development.[44] Trekking, on the other hand, is a sporting activity that involves long walks in nature, alone or in a group, and represents a concentration of emotional, ecological and novelty values.[45]

Although the concept of slow tourism is relatively new and there is a dearth of literature about it, it is possible to compare different authors' explanations of it. According to Moore,[46] the two driving forces of slow tourism are environmental sustainability and personal/social well-being. Social well-being refers to the idea that not only the tourist can benefit from his holiday; restaurants, locals and the environment are fundamental actors that can take advantage of a holiday as well as tourists. Instead, Parkins and Craig[47] believe that the focus of slow tourism in recent years has been shifting from mere environmental sustainability to the practice of time and space that leads to personal satisfaction and well-being. Again, according to Yurtseven and Kaya,[48] the two principles of slow tourism are taking time and exploring an attachment to a particular place. Caffyn[49] provides a more categorical definition of slow tourism. First, slow tourism has the following key dimensions: place (locality, distinctiveness, heritage, environment), people (community, culture, cuisine), time (pace, relaxation), travel (distance, emissions) and the personal (well-being, pleasure, learning, enjoyment). Second, it features the following basic elements:

- Minimizing travel distance, at least by car or by plane
- Maximizing the time available for the trip
- Relaxing and refreshing both the mind and the body
- Exploring the local area in depth; seeking out the distinctiveness
- Being in contact with local people, cultures, communities and heritage
- Eating at local restaurants; trying local drinks, beer, wine
- Learning new skills or engaging in new activities
- Minimizing one's carbon footprint
- Experiencing authenticity
- Shopping in local markets or directly from producers
- Minimizing use of technology

This list cannot be considered exhaustive, but the more of these elements that are present, the slower a holiday might be judged to be. Furthermore, they can vary enormously from location to location.

According to Caffyn, destinations also play an important role in slow tourism. Indeed, if they are not able to promote and facilitate this kind of tourism, slow tourists will find it difficult to organize their trip, or they will not choose that particular destination for their holiday. For this reason, in addition to the principles of slow tourism, Caffyn also provided a list of actions that destinations should take in order to promote slow holidays. To start, destinations should highlight slow arrival methods, such as public transport or car sharing. They should also tackle infrastructure issues that make slow choices more difficult. For instance, encouraging train companies to allow more bicycles on board or encouraging them to offer free bike tickets is a good starting point, especially for people who love cycling. They can also promote the use of slower transport options during the holiday, such as offering discounts for those arriving without a car or by keeping visitors engaged within a short distance of their accommodations with attractive activities. In addition, destinations or accommodations can encourage longer stays by suggesting itineraries, activities and packages to their customers. In fact, some hotels require a minimum stay of two or three nights, sending their guests a list of all the possible activities to do around the hotel to discourage them from only staying for a single night. Slow activities include walking, cycling and riding routes, rowing boats or tasting sessions. Hotels and info-points should inform tourists about all of these opportunities to grant them a relaxing stay and, at the same time, to make them more involved. Moreover, all of these activities are environmentally friendly, which is one of the goals of slow tourism. Viewpoints, outdoor cafes and picnic sites can be good solutions for enjoying nature in slower environments such as tranquil parks or mobile phone free zones. In terms of food, destinations should support local food and drink, especially by promoting of local events, festivals and traditions. In this way, tourists will be able to discover local products and have contact with local producers, potentially with the opportunity to learn how the final product they're enjoying is obtained. In addition, restaurants should offer their guests traditional dishes, tastings and fair trade products. Caffyn also believes that it is important to allow visitors to choose their own pace — for example, by having flexible timings for meals or options to extend stays. Finally, to guarantee these services to tourists, local agents have to invest in their staff to ensure that they are not only skilled but also have good knowledge of the local area and are willing and able to share this knowledge with visitors.

Importantly, Dickinson and Lumsdon argue that any definition of slow tourism should take into consideration transportation for the sake of environmental protection.[50] Furthermore, they define slow tourism as a

> conceptual framework that involves people who travel to destinations more slowly overland, stay longer and travel less and who incorporate travel to a destination as itself an experience and, once at the destination, engage with local transport options and slow food and beverage, take time to explore local history and culture, and support the environment.[51]

As we can see, time and environment are the two core elements of a slow holiday. Indeed, slow tourists are known to stay longer than other tourists in their chosen destination, which gives them more opportunities to interact with the local population and to share moments, culture and heritage. Thus, Georgica stated that slow tourism is about becoming a part of the local life of the destination that consumers visit.[52]

Proximity tourism is related to slow tourism. It is a form of territorial tourism that has as its goal the exploration of destinations close to where you live. Moreover, it is a form of sustainable tourism that focuses on enhancing one's territorial heritage. The territorial heritage of proximity is the set of components of cultural heritage, both material and intangible, that tend to be of little value when considered exclusively from an economic perspective; therefore, it is fragile. This fragility can lead to the degradation, loss and abandonment of such assets, hence the importance of supporting enhancement processes that, in turn, can trigger local development.[53] Local resources represent the starting point for developing a place's specific tourist products; the elements of differentiation between various localities include natural attractions, cultural elements, history and local folklore.[54] Increasing the attractiveness of a region can be pursued by leveraging typical lifestyle elements and local traditions, highlighting its authenticity and, therefore, increasing its uniqueness. Achieving a promotional return in favour of local tourism and the image of the host city is often encouraged by the creation of events (food and wine, sports, art, etc.). The aggregative events highlight the desire to territorialize culture, reinventing the authenticity of places for visitors. Cultural events, integrated with food and wine resources, is one of the most widespread interorganizational forms in local tourism policies.[55]

3.5 Analysis of the effects of COVID-19 on the Italian tourism sector

Tourism is one of the fastest-growing and most significant industries in Italy, and it has proven to be a valuable economic pillar of the Italian economy. Its long-term development potential is important, as businesses and public and private organizations are strongly interested in the economic impacts of tourism at national and regional levels. Like many other Organization for Economic Cooperation and Development (OECD) countries, Italy and its regions face a range of challenges and opportunities to maintain or transform their natural, historical and cultural assets into a thriving, sustainable tourism destinations, which could help support local economic growth. Italy's geographic location, as well as its historic heritage, offers a wealth of scenic views that attract both locals and foreigners to participate in tourism-related activities. Fifth in the world and third in Europe in terms of international tourist arrivals, Italy attracts millions of tourists every year thanks to its fascinating culture, natural landscapes, artistic sites and renowned cuisine.[56]

Data published by the World Travel & Tourism Council in 2019 show the leading role that the tourism sector plays in Italy's economy.[57] As of 2019, the tourism industry was responsible for over 1.5

million jobs in Italy, and, according to forecasts, this figure was expected to rise steadily until 2029. According to the Italian National Institute of Statistics (ISTAT), the number of international tourist arrivals in Italy rose from about 81.6 million tourists in 2015 to roughly 96 million in 2019. When looking at the most popular destinations, the ISTAT reveals that Rome, Venice, Milan and Florence were the leading municipalities by the number of overnight stays as of 2018. In fact, a recent study included Rome and Milan in a list of the leading European tourism destinations by the number of overnight stays in 2018. Moreover, as confirmed by the arrivals of roughly 4.6 million domestic tourists, the Italian capital was very popular among national travellers too.

This situation has changed rapidly with the arrival of COVID-19. The rapid spread of the novel coronavirus, since the first case occurred in December 2019 in Wuhan, Mainland China, definitely led to a devastating impact on the global economy, in particular on the tourism sector, which has been strongly affected by the measures that were taken to contain the pandemic. It will be very difficult for the situation to return to normal in the short term. Even if tourism has shown a great capacity for change in the past few decades, today it is unfortunately one of the economic sectors most affected by the epidemic, and it has suffered significant losses on all fronts.[58] Unfortunately, many businesses in the tourism sector did not survive. Those that managed to stay operational, even after a slowdown in containment measures, face the challenges of a probable slow recovery.

As one of the main outbreak areas, Italy has been affected in a very deep way by the virus from the point of view of both the health system due to the high number of infections and the economic system due to the closure of multiple activities.[59] Three specific factors related to the epidemic have had the strongest negative effects on tourism: official travel restrictions, event cancellations (trade fairs, congresses, conferences, cultural and sporting events, etc.) and travellers' fear of risk.[60] Therefore, the big picture of the tourism industry during the pandemic is dramatic: hotels and other accommodations have been closed, airlines have reduced their flights drastically, cruise lines have suspended travel, restaurants have either restricted their activities or relied exclusively on delivery services, and few people have participated in leisure and entertainment activities. Considering the size and dynamics of the global tourism market, the cancellation of flights and holidays and the geographical spread of COVID-19 and its potential economic impact, the World Tourism Organization has slowly reevaluated the consequences of the crisis on international tourism.[61] During the last decade, the estimated growth rate for arrivals in 2020 was 3%–4%. However, at the end of March 2020, the forecast shows a dramatic 20%–30% decrease in international tourists.

In the housing and food services sectors, 51 million businesses are facing an extraordinarily difficult business environment with huge impacts on opportunities for employment. People who work in the tourism industry are facing job losses, reductions in paid time at work and other work-related challenges, due to the drastic fall in economic activity. Independent workers and small companies together represent 60% of the accommodation and food services subsectors, and they are especially fragile in relation to the economic crisis. For instance, since governments required the closure of all non-essential businesses, a lot of companies had no choice but to reduce their operational expenditures.[62] Civil aviation, craft industry, agriculture, and food and beverage supply have all been seriously damaged. Cumulative, objective (closing borders, travel bans, confinement and quarantine measures) and subjective (behavioural) factors have led to a decline in the number of arrivals (between 290 and 440 million) and in revenue of $300–450 billion (out of a total of about $1500 billion annually).

A recent forecast study predicted that tourists' behaviour will change drastically and that many people, even after the restrictions are lifted, will continue to renounce to travel for a long time. In terms of the specific acts that affected Italy's economy, tourists were blocked and prevented from entering the country to contain the spread of the virus.[63] Although since February 2020, when the pandemic started spreading, many people stopped travelling, it was only at the beginning of March 2020 when Italy zeroed in on travel restrictions in line with the generalized measures of social distancing, tourism came to a standstill.[64] The northern part of the country (Lombardy, Veneto and Emilia Romagna) lost 11,779,530 arrivals in the lockdown period. According to Confturismo, Italy's Tourism Association, the number of tourists entering the country between March and May was 30 million, which was fewer than anticipated.[65] In March 2020 alone, almost 90% of hotel and travel agency bookings for Rome were cancelled and 80% were cancelled for Sicily.

During the pandemic, international tourists' expenditures in Italy decreased significantly. Spending in March 2019 was $2.9 billion, while in March 2020, it dropped to $478 million. In April 2020, it hit an all-time low at 4,350 million. In August 2021, these numbers seemed to be recovering, as incoming tourism expenditures reached $5.3 billion, well over 2020 levels but not yet equal to 2019, where it amounted to $5.7 billion.[66]

Normally, Italy has a positive tourist balance. In 2019, this trend continued, as international tourists entering Italy spent more than Italian travellers abroad. In July 2019, the difference in spending was more than $3 billion. In March 2020, due to the coronavirus pandemic and the closure of the borders, Italy had a negative tourist balance of $100 million dollars, and a negative figure was also reported the following month. In the summers of 2020 and 2021, Italy's tourism balance turned positive, settling at $2.9 billion in August 2021.[67] The regions most affected by COVID-19 are the northern regions, especially Lombardy and Veneto, where the first cases of COVID-19 in the country appeared and where the first lockdowns were implemented.[68]

The economic vulnerability of the tourism market, particularly as it is driven by tourists' demand, impacts small and medium-sized enterprises (SMEs) especially, which could have negative effects for the labour market.[69] There will be also consequences for tourist offerings, employee incomes and economically weak communities that rely on tourism for their survival. The economic impact for destinations will depend upon several factors, including the impact of travel restrictions on visitor flow, the nature of their tourism offers, the velocity with which the economy gathers up in source markets and the size of the domestic tourism market and exposure to the global marketplace.[70] It is extremely difficult to predict what the real impact of the pandemic will be on tourism because the time and space dimensions cannot be foreseen and the effects are difficult to quantify.[71] What is certain is that the pandemic undeniably represents an important watershed moment for tourism: this is how tourism was before COVID-19, and this is how tourism will be once the emergency is over and mobility modes and behaviours are forever changed.[72] Decision-makers around the world have been trying to find ways to mitigate the economic impact of the pandemic, but recovery cannot begin until the health emergency is under control and travel restrictions can be lifted safely.[73]

3.6 Adaptation of the tourism sector to COVID-19: a resilient approach

In terms of scale, scope and trajectory, the COVID-19 crisis has impacted the tourism sector in a way that no previous crises ever did before.[74] Historically, demand is known to rebound after a crisis, although the recovery time and profile vary. Analysis by McKinsey shows that after SARS (2003) and MERS (2015), it took between three and five months to recover to pre-crisis levels of demand. Currently, the information available is insufficient to make reliable predictions concerning the geographical and temporal distribution and intensity (in terms of morbidity and mortality) of the global pandemic.[75] In the absence of such predictions, the uncertain cycle and global nature of the pandemic puts the industry in a unique situation, especially because an end date is harder to predict, and the pervasiveness of the virus leaves few options for travellers and operators. The current state of recession, especially in the tourism industry, requires rethinking and implementing new development models based on safety practices that protect travellers and all people, support sustainability and reduce the impact on environmental and cultural resources, as set out in the objectives of the UN's 2030 Agenda.

With the World Health Organization's (WHO) declaration of the pandemic, most tourist activities stopped, causing a change in people's behaviours and consciousness so much that a "new normal" based on new economic, social and cultural values is being created. The "new normal" cannot be reduced to strengthening healthcare systems or restoring economic balance; it must be a complete redesign of the models we use to offer and understand tourism. Many countries are now entering a new phase in fighting the virus while simultaneously managing the re-opening of their tourist economy.[76] Travel constraints and special provisions to contain the pandemic will most likely be in place for a long time and will only be gradually reduced. Government support in the first phase of the crisis was focused on immediate response and mitigation efforts to protect visitors and workers and ensure business continuity following the imposition of containment measures. While the medium and long-term impacts of COVID-19 on tourism will vary among countries, destinations and sector segments, it is clear that in order to open up while the virus continues to circulate, governments will need to take balanced, measured and coordinated policy action at the local, national and international level in order to protect people while minimizing job losses and business closures.

While country response measures continue to focus on public health issues, governments have also moved quickly to introduce extraordinary initiatives to mitigate the economic impact of the coronavirus on businesses and workers. For instance, the Italian government has employed a range of instruments to support operators in the travel and tourism sector.[77] Government assistance efforts include communication campaigns to help prevent the spread of the virus; the provision of flexibility and relief for companies and workers hurt by reduced demand, temporary lay-offs and sick leave; and, liquidity injections and other financial instruments (e.g., tax relief, guarantees, grants, tax holidays or postponements, etc.) to ensure business survival in the immediate term. Governments have taken unprecedented steps to respond to the crisis at a sectorial level with creative solutions to support tourism businesses and workers, restore travellers' confidence and be ready to stimulate demand once containment measures are lifted.

Such actions are essential, but to reopen the tourism economy successfully and get businesses up and running, more needs to be done in a coordinated way, as tourism services are very interdependent. For this purpose, the Council of Ministers, taking into account the numerous instances promoted by the trade associations, has launched a series of extraordinary measures to support workers and enterprises in the tourism and cultural sectors with a regulatory act called "Cura Italia". This legislative Act had provided special allowances for workers in the tourism, entertainment and cultural sectors, which have also been extended to workers without social security benefits. In addition, companies operating in the tourism sector have been temporarily exempted from the payment of withholding taxes, social security contributions and compulsory insurance premiums. Moreover, the Act has provided refunds with vouchers both to reimburse tourists who have seen travel and packages cancelled as a result of the COVID-19 emergency and for hotels and other accommodation facilities.

From a social point of view, the lockdown imposed on Italians has completely changed the daily life of people and families, who have had to learn to live with new habits and to put on hold the frenetic lifestyles that typically characterize our accelerated society. To support Italians through this delicate period, the Ministry for Cultural Heritage and Activities and the Ministry for Tourism launched a "Culture does not stop" initiative to allow citizens, forced to stay at home, to live virtual tourist experiences through digital tours, YouTube videos, 3D playback or online visits in augmented reality.

The COVID-19 emergency has also made evident how new digital media (apps, artificial intelligence, augmented reality, Internet of Things, etc.) are important for users not only in terms of communication and entertainment but also in terms of the redefinition of daily life.[78] In this specific case, the possibilities that new technologies offer to practice virtual tourism have given people the opportunity to distract themselves during quarantine, offering the impression of full immersion in places that are physically far away but feel as close as ever.

As the effects of the pandemic unfold, there are some recommendations and advice for responding to the structural changes that are underway in the tourism sector. The crisis resulting from the pandemic is not just a problem; it can also be seen as an opportunity. It can lead to a rethinking of tourism in a more sustainable guise.[79] To address this situation, political interventions will be necessary to encourage the use of new business models, embrace digitization and promote territorial tourism.[80] The latter will be the key in an after-crisis scenario where social distancing remains relevant and tourists seek out less crowded destinations.[81] Tourism consists of both a dynamic (transportation) and a non-dynamic (accommodation) component; these are the two main areas that must be heavily adapted and transformed to comply with serious health safety measures in order to convince people to keep travelling and going on holidays. If travellers are assured that their means of transportation and their destination accommodation will protect them from the virus, then they can self-isolate during holidays and enjoy a more independent style of tourism, maintaining all of the safety measures and precautions that they also practice at home. The safety needs of visitors and guests require an additional dose of empathy, reassurance and goodwill.

Some also propose taking advantage of the crisis to make structural changes in tourism (although defining concrete strategies for doing so remains complex given the high degree of uncertainty), betting on a future model where priority is given to local tourism based on a greater integration of the tourist with the territory and its values.[82] Sustainability should be a guiding principle in recovery, supporting the aim of limiting tourism's role as a vector of the pandemic[83] (e.g., issues related to waste management). Support and recovery measures need to be comprehensive across the sector branches that make up the tourism experience. Accessibility, connectivity and transport should be as high on the agenda as accommodations, restaurants, resorts, events, travel association, travel tech companies, tour operators and tourism associations. It is very likely that some of the sudden, emergency changes imposed during the pandemic will remain (if not in full, at least in part) as common practices in post-COVID-19 society.[84]

While the focus in recent months has rightly been on protecting workers and visitors and supporting business survival, policy makers also need to consider the longer-term implications of COVID-19 on tourism and the innovations that will be needed to build a stronger, more sustainable and more resilient tourism economy in the future.[85] The measures put in place today will shape the tourism of tomorrow. Looking ahead, governments need to consider the longer-term implications of the crisis, while staying ahead of the digital curve, supporting the low carbon transition and promoting the structural transformation needed to build a more sustainable and resilient tourism economy. Beyond immediate responses, policy makers will need to learn from the lessons of the COVID-19 crisis to improve crisis management strategies and better prepare destinations and the sector more broadly to respond to future shocks. Adopting a resilient approach is valuable for evaluating the effective impact of the pandemic dynamics, and it is necessary to provide support tools for decision-makers in order to be prepared for the unexpected and to adapt smartly.[86]

Resilience theory postulates that change is fundamental and is the only constant that everyone can depend on.[87] Of course, it is not possible to draw up general rules that apply to everyone in all circumstances, as strategies are, by definition, conditioned by the history and characteristics of individual enterprises. However, it is possible to outline some priorities that companies in the tourism sector should take seriously when defining their strategies.[88] Faced with uncertainty, companies could take a very risky "wait-and-see" attitude. However, in this context, consumers appreciate companies that are proactive, give strong signals, propose immediate solutions for the most recurring doubts and anticipate customer requests when possible.[89] To this end, it may be useful to take advantage of the opportunities granted by smart work to keep customer support services active and to feed all communication channels (website, chat, social pages, call centre, messaging applications, etc.). Moreover, every possible relaunch strategy must involve guaranteeing maximum health and safety conditions. This is an obvious goal, but it is not trivial, as the holiday is also etymologically associated with the concept of freedom and little is compatible with the presence of a series of constraints that inevitably risk drastically impoverishing the tourist experience. In this sense, companies in the sector are called upon to make a creative effort to rethink the experiences they offer their customers from an innovative perspective where points of weakness imposed by unexpected circumstances can become new opportunities.

As analysed, chaos can rapidly envelop tourism activities due to the complexity of the systems and their inherent vulnerability to external threats, in this case, the COVID-19 pandemic.[90] Resilience thinking is valuable for addressing uncertainty. Identifying and addressing complex unknowns, however, is a major challenge, both for academics and for tourism practitioners. In this stormy moment, it is important to maintain a certain perspective: history shows that tragic events happen, but human beings come together, and innovation increases, solutions are found and society advances.[91] Therefore, it is important to take the opportunity offered by this global pause to rethink the future of tourism, following the inspiration of Taleb Rifai's final words as United Nations World Tourism Organization (UNWTO) Secretary-General: *"Whatever our business in life may be, let us always remember that our core business is, and will always be, to make this world a better place".*[92]

3.7 Expected future trends on the tourism industry & consumer perspectives

One significant change that can be observed in the public domain is the very active and widespread engagement with the question of what the future will look like after the threat of the virus has subsided. These range from predictions about the depth and length of the economic depression to calls to action that see the disruption caused by COVID-19 as an opportunity to redirect society's developmental path.[93] It is extremely difficult to predict which trends in the tourism industry will continue into the future, but what is certain is that the coronavirus pandemic is, first and foremost, a humanitarian crisis that is affecting people's lives and has triggered a global economic crisis. The tourism sector is living through a difficult moment to rethink tourist activity, tourism planning, management and destination development based on a new humanism that would consider the "human factor" more than it has done so far. When the "war" against the COVID-19 is won, the pandemic will leave behind a long trail of changes in personal and professional lives.

In the context of this radical uncertainty, research centres, institutions and trade associations are converging in their expectations about some future trends. First, domestic tourism will most likely recover before international tourism does. This is not only because nations will lift their internal bans earlier but also because of the perception of greater safety and greater reliability that tourists will have travelling within their country. The expectation is that domestic travel in Italy will reach 2019 levels in 2022, while international travel in Italy will not reach 2019 levels until at least the following year. Second, impacts will not be the same for everyone: the destinations that are largely dependent on long-haul foreign markets will be the most affected by the effects of this crisis. The destinations most visited by domestic tourists or those from neighbouring countries will be able to recover faster and will be less affected by the pandemic. Another future perspective is that the recovery will be slow. Despite the industry's proven resilience in response to previous crises, the magnitude of the impact of the COVID-19 will put a strain on the industry and make it difficult to recover quickly. The current pandemic is global and will, according to current estimates, cover a much longer period of time than previous crises, which have been much more localized and limited in terms of their effects on tourism. Moreover, irrespective of the ongoing battle against COVID-19, mass tourism has been hit forever.

Mass tourism as a model had already started to change before COVID-19 because many contemporary travellers seek unique experiences and started rejecting the all-inclusive packages model in the 1980s and 1990s. Independent tourism had already started taking over, both due to an attitude change in the culture and the education of travellers, but it has also turned out that independent tourism is safer. Previously overcrowded destinations might see high reductions in tourist flows, as rural, less crowded destinations simultaneously become more popular. Some Italian regions, for example, want to promote cultural tourism by exploiting lesser-known UNESCO heritage sites that are close to places of great attraction. Popular destinations may also need to reconfigure their development model to attract people while ensuring sufficient social distancing.

The coronavirus will also help to combat over-tourism, a concept that refers to a situation in which tourist numbers are so high that they go beyond the capacity (environmental, social and economic dimensions) of a particular destination.[94] Reversing over-tourism, creating social distance to prevent the spreading of viruses and imposing safety distances between tourists in crowded places will eventually mitigate the problem of over-tourism through the reduction of the tourist numbers. Thus, environmental sustainability will also be promoted. In recent years, corporate sustainability has assumed increasing importance within the business community, and many of the leading players in the tourism industry have pursued sustainability programs designed to incorporate environmental, social, economic and governance issues into their business strategies.[95] This period must be used in a meaningful way to reflect on tourism and on the necessary structural changes that sustainable development strategies require.[96] As authors such as Fletcher et al. suggested,

> even if the COVID-19 crisis ends relatively soon, we cannot afford to return to levels of travel experienced previously, particularly by the wealthiest segment of the world's population. This is not only because of the social unrest over tourism provoked, but also because the industry's environmental damages (including climate change as well as pollution and resource depletion) which were already beyond unsustainable.[97]

Furthermore, as Cohen argued,

> COVID-19 is an opportunity to reduce over the longer term the prevalence of lifestyles premised on large volumes of energy and material throughput.... policy makers it should create the conditions that allow the coronavirus epidemic to facilitate a sustainable consumption transition.[98]

This transition requires significant changes in the current business models and strategies of many companies in the tourism sector.

The COVID-19 situation has forced tourism businesses to face new and very complex challenges. However, it has paved the way for new changes and new links between tourism and sustainable development. It has highlighted some of the inherent contradictions and complexities within the concept of sustainable development, and it has offered some radical solutions to the challenges of sustainability. All stakeholders, including researchers, have a very important task: to bring tourism, both on the supply side and on the demand side, in the direction of sustainability and resilience, capable of moving towards a future of continuous evolution and many new challenges.[99] Moreover, one of the necessary future challenges will be to encourage digitization and digital literacy in order to foster the union of tradition and innovation, since new technologies are gradually gaining their place in tourism as in many other economic sectors.[100] Virtual reality in the tourism sector is an option that should be paid renewed attention, not in an attempt to replace real tourism but to complement it and replace or complement realistic experiences that are perilous.

The COVID-19 pandemic will probably be the toughest stress test ever for the entire tourism industry, and, when it is over, everyone will surely find a changed industry, on both the demand and supply sides. The characteristics of the COVID-19 emergency, which have resulted in a permanent paralysis of global tourism, have also led tourism businesses and destinations to adjust their offers to respond to changed travel behaviours. The pandemic has indeed given consumers the time and opportunity to reflect on the basic meaning of consumption and the impact of their consumption not just on themselves, but also on others, society and the environment.[101] In particular, an interesting question arises: During the post-pandemic era, what will the new trends in travel be? In other words, what potential new tourism behaviours will emerge? Will consumers need to resort to their own moral judgements when deciding whether, when and how to travel?[102] Predicting the trajectory of changes in tourist behaviour is essential for helping tourism managers identify the basis of a resilience strategy to ideally respond to the situation.[103] That is why this empirical study was conducted to understand tourists' sensitivity to health crises like the coronavirus with the aim of identifying any potential changes in tourists' consumption as a consequence of COVID-19.

Notes

1 World Travel &Tourism Council, Economic Impact Reports, 2021.
2 World Tourism Organization, 2021, https://www.unwto.org/news/global-tourism-sees-upturn-in-q3-but-recovery-remains-fragile
3 Ali Y., Ciaschini M., Pretaroli R., Severini F., Socci C., "Economic relevance of tourism industry: The Italian case", *Quaderno di Dipartimento*, No. 72, 2014.
4 Robinson P., Heitmann S., Dieke P., *Research themes for tourism*, Wallingford, Oxfordshire; Cambridge, MA: CABI, 2011
5 Ueli G., "The history of tourism: Structures on the path to modernity", *European History Online*, 2010; MacKenzie N.G., Pittaki Z., Wong N., "Historical approaches for hospitality and tourism research", *International Journal of Contemporary Hospitality Management*, Vol. 32 No. 4, 2020, pp. 1469–1485.
6 Eccles G., Costa J., "Perspectives on tourism development", *International Journal of Contemporary Hospitality Management*, Vol. 8 No. 7, 1996, pp. 44–51.

7 Korstanje M.E., "Touring beyond the nation: A transnational approach to European tourism history", *International Journal of Culture, Tourism and Hospitality Research*, Vol. 7 No. 4, 2013, pp. 425–427.

8 Baum T., "Images of tourism past and present", *International Journal of Contemporary Hospitality Management*, Vol. 8 No. 4, 1996, pp. 25–30.

9 Camilleri M.A., "The tourism industry: An overview", in *Travel marketing, tourism economics and the airline product* (Chapter 1, pp. 3–27). Cham, Switzerland: Springer Nature, 2018.

10 Uriely N., "Deconstructing tourist typologies: The case of backpacking", *International Journal of Culture, Tourism and Hospitality Research*, Vol. 3 No. 4, 2009, pp. 306–312.

11 Russo A.P., "The 'vicious circle' of tourism development in heritage cities", *Annals of Tourism Research*, Vol. 29 No. 1, 2002, pp. 165–182.

12 Kladou S., Giannopoulos A., Assiouras I., "Matching tourism type and destination image perceptions in a country context", *Journal of Place Management and Development*, Vol. 7 No. 2, 2014, pp. 141–152.

13 Camilleri M.A., op. cit.

14 Knetsch J.L., Var, T., "The impacts of tourism and recreational facility development", *The Tourist Review*, Vol. 31 No. 4, 1976, pp. 5–10.

15 Slocum S., Everett S., "Industry, government, and community: Power and leadership in a resource constrained DMO", *Tourism Review*, Vol. 69 No. 1, 2014, pp. 47–58.

16 Zalatan A., Ramirez Gaston A., "Soft ecotourism: The substitution effect", *The Tourist Review*, Vol. 51 No. 4, 1996, pp. 42–48; Duong N.T.H., Chi N.K., Nguyen H.T., Nguyen N.T.K., Nguyen C.P., Nguyen U.T.T., "WTPP for ecotourism: The impact of intention, perceived value, and materialism", *Journal of Hospitality and Tourism Insights*, ahead-of-print, 2021.

17 Pralong J., "Geotourism: A new form of tourism utilising natural landscapes and based on imagination and emotion", *Tourism Review*, Vol. 61, No. 3, 2006, pp. 20–25.

18 Skuras D., Castro Caldas J., Meccheri N., Psaltopoulos D., Viladomiu L., "Institutional support to strategic business orientations: An empirical analysis of rural businesses in four countries of southern Europe", *European Business Review*, Vol. 15 No. 4, 2003, pp. 235–244.

19 Swart M.P., "Proposing an experiential value model within the context of business tourism", inSotiriadis M., Gursoy D. (Eds.), *The handbook of managing and marketing tourism experiences*. Bingley: Emerald Group Publishing Limited, 2016, pp. 451–468.

20 Wong B.K.M., Sa'aid Hazley S.A., "The future of health tourism in the industrial revolution 4.0 era", *Journal of Tourism Futures*, Vol. 7 No. 2, 2021, pp. 267–272; Aydin G., Karamehmet B., "Factors affecting health tourism and international health-care facility choice", *International Journal of Pharmaceutical and Healthcare Marketing*, Vol. 11 No. 1, 2017, pp. 16–36.

21 Vlahovi D., "Original culture in the development of contemporary tourism", *The Tourist Review*, Vol. 55 No. 4, 2000, pp. 23–31.

22 Cugini A., "Religious tourism and sustainability: From devotion to spiritual experience", in Grasso F., Sergi B.S. (Eds.), *Tourism in the*

Mediterranean Sea. Bingley: Emerald Publishing Limited, 2021, pp. 55–73.

23 Romanelli M., Gazzola P., Grechi D., Pollice F., "Towards a sustainability-oriented religious tourism", *Systems Research and Behavioral Science*, Vol. 38 No. 3, 2021, pp. 386–396.

24 Ingram H., "Classification and grading of smaller hotels, guesthouses and bed and breakfast accommodation", *International Journal of Contemporary Hospitality Management*, Vol. 8 No. 5, 1996, pp. 30–34.

25 Schuckert M., Peters M., Fessler B., "An empirical assessment of owner-manager motives in the B&B and vacation home sector", *Tourism Review*, Vol. 63 No. 4, 2008, pp. 27–39.

26 Grando S., Bartolini F., Bonjean I., Brunori G., Mathijs E., Prosperi P., Vergamini D., "Small farms' behaviour: Conditions, strategies and performances", in Brunori G., Grando S. (Eds.), *Innovation for sustainability (research in rural sociology and development)*, Vol. 25. Bingley: Emerald Publishing Limited, 2020, pp. 125–169.

27 Pröbstl-Haider U., Melzer V., Jiricka A., "Rural tourism opportunities: Strategies and requirements for destination leadership in peripheral areas", *Tourism Review*, Vol. 69 No. 3, 2014, pp. 216–228.

28 Scaglione M., Larpin B., Johnson C., "Airbnb's guests' rating of host's professional qualities", in Chen J.S. (Ed.), *Advances in hospitality and leisure (advances in hospitality and leisure)*, Vol. 17. Bingley: Emerald Publishing Limited, 2021, pp. 55–83.

29 Dredge D., Gyimothy S., "Collaborative economy and tourism: Critical perspectives, questionable claims and silenced voices", *Tourism Recreation Research*, Vol. 40 No. 3, 2015, pp. 286–302.

30 Birinci H., Berezina K. Cobanoglu C., "Comparing customer perceptions of hotel and peer-to-peer accommodation advantages and disadvantages", *International Journal of Contemporary Hospitality Management*, Vol. 30 No. 2, 2018, pp. 1190–1210.

31 Pavione E., Pezzetti R., "Evolution of tourism demand and development of sustainable tourism: What impact on tourist destinations?", Strategica International Academic Conference 2016, Opportunities & Risks in the Contemporary Business Environment, College of Management, National University of Political Studies and Public Administration, Bucharest, Romania, October 20–21, 2016.

32 Niininen O., Buhalis D., March R., "Customer empowerment in tourism through consumer centric marketing (CCM)", *Qualitative Market Research*, Vol. 10 No. 3, 2007, pp. 265–281.

33 Smith V.L., Eadington W.R., *Tourism alternatives: Potentials and problems in the development of tourism*, Philadelphia: University of Pennsylvania Press, 1992.

34 Calzati V., *Nuove pratiche turistiche e slow tourism. Il caso della Valnerina in Umbria*. Milano: Franco Angeli, 2016.

35 Franch M., Martini U., Buffa F., Parisi G., "4L tourism (landscape, leisure, learning, and limit): Responding to new motivations and expectations of tourists to improve the competitivness of Alpine destinations in a sustainable way", *Tourism Review*, Vol. 63 No. 1, 2008, pp. 4–14.

36 United Nations Environment Programme World Tourism Organization, *Making tourism more sustainable: A guide for policy makers*. New York: United Nations Publications, 2005.

37 Over time, various definitions of sustainable tourism have been developed, all of which are however linked to the more general definition of sustainable development. The World Tourism & Travel Council in 1996 defined sustainable tourism as a form of tourism that "works for the regeneration and future productivity of natural resources; recognizes the contribution to the tourist experience of populations, communities, customs and lifestyles". WWF emphasizes environmental values, defining sustainable tourism as a tourism capable of lasting over time, maintaining its qualitative and quantitative values, that is, capable of making the expectations of residents coincide in the short and long term with those of tourists, without decreasing the qualitative level of the tourist experience and without damaging the environmental values of the territory affected by the phenomenon. The Cape Town Declaration on Responsible Tourism of 2012 identifies responsible tourism in some salient features: the minimization of the environmental impact, the creation of economic benefits for the host community, the involvement of the local population, the conservation of natural heritage and cultural.

38 Weaver D.B., *Sustainable tourism*. New York: Routledge, 2006; Goodwin H., Francis J., "Ethical and responsible tourism: Consumer trend in the UK", *Journal of Vacation Marketing*, Vol. 9 No. 3, 2003, pp. 271–284; Buckley R., "Sustainable tourism: Research and reality", *Annals of Tourism Research*, Vol. 39 No. 2, 2012, pp. 528–546; Butler R.W., "Sustainable tourism: A state of the art review", *Tourism Geographies*, Vol. 1 No. 1, 1999, pp. 7–25; Frey N., George R., "Responsible tourism management: The missing link between business owners' attitudes and behaviour in the Cape Town tourism industry", *Tourism Management*, Vol. 31 No. 5, 2010, pp. 621–628; Sin H.L., "Who are we responsible to? Locals' talent of volunteer tourism", *Geoforum*, Vol. 41, 2010, pp. 983–992; Caruana R., Glozer S., Crane A., Mccabe S., "Tourists' accounts of responsible tourism", *Annals of Tourism Research*, Vol. 46, 2014, pp. 115–129; Mahrouse G., "Feel-good tourism: An ethical option for socially-conscious westerners?", *ACME*, Vol. 10 No. 3, 2011, pp. 372–391.

39 World Tourism Organization, *The British ecotourism market*. Madrid: World Tourism Organization, 2001.

40 Stronza A.L., Hunt C.A., Fitzgerald L.A., "Ecotourism for conservation?", *Annual Review of Environment and Resources*, Vol. 44 No. 1, 2019, pp. 229–253.

41 Fadini S., "Il turismo responsabile e il rapporto coi residenti", *Rivista di Scienze del Turismo – Ambiente Cultura Diritto Economia*, Vol. 4 No. 1–2, 2018, pp. 83–102.

42 Robinson P., Heitmann S., Dieke P., *Research themes for tourism*. Wallingford: CAB International, 2011.

43 Pavione E., Pezzetti R., "The valorisation of 'slow territories' through the development of sustainable and experiential tourism", Strategica

International Academic Conference 2016, Opportunities & Risks in the Contemporary Business Environment, College of Management, National University of Political Studies and Public Administration in Romania Bucharest, Romania, October 20–21, 2016.

44 Gazzola P., Pavione E., Grechi D., Ossola P., "Cycle tourism as a driver for the sustainable development of little-known or remote territories: The experience of the Appennine Regions of Northern Italy", *Sustainability (Basel, Switzerland)*, Vol. 10 No. 6, 2018, p. 1863.

45 Lee S.A., Manthiou A., Chiang L., Tang L.R., "An assessment of value dimensions in hiking tourism: Pathways toward quality of life", *The International Journal of Tourism Research*, Vol. 20 No. 2, 2018, pp. 236–246.

46 Moore K., *On the periphery of pleasure: Hedonics, eudaimonics, and slow travel, slow tourism: Experiences and mobilities.* Bristol: Channel View Publications Ltd, 2012, pp. 25–35.

47 Parkins W., Craig G., *Slow living.* Oxford: Berg Publishers, 2006.

48 Yurtseven H.R., Kaya O., "Slow tourists: A comparative research based on cittaslow principles", *American International Journal of Contemporary Research*, Vol. 1 No. 2, 2011, pp. 91–98.

49 Caffyn A., "Advocating and implementing slow tourism", *Tourism Recreation Research*, Vol. 37 No. 1, 2012, pp. 77–80.

50 Dickinson J., Lumsdon L., *Slow travel and tourism.* London: Earthscan Ltd, 2010.

51 Dickinson J., Lumsdon L., op. cit., pp. 1–2.

52 Georgica G., "The tourist's perception about slow travel: a Romanian perspective", *Procedia Economics and Finance*, 23, 2015, pp. 1596–1601.

53 Buratti N., Ferrari C., *La valorizzazione del patrimonio di prossimità tra fragilità e sviluppo locale. Un approccio multidisciplinare.* Milano: Franco Angeli, 2011.

54 Ferrari S., Adamo E.G., "Autenticità e risorse locali come attrattive turistiche: il caso della Calabria", *Sinergie Rivista Di Studi e Ricerche*, No. 66, 2005, pp. 79–112.

55 Costa N., *I professionisti dello sviluppo turistico locale. I sistemi turistici locali come opportunità di lavoro.* Milano: Hoepli, 2005.

56 Alberici A., Tourism and economic dimension in Italy, Dep. Econ. Univ. Milan Italy, Departmental Working Papers, January 2007.

57 World Travel & Tourism Council, Country Data, Regional Overview, 2019.

58 Folinas S., Metaxas T., Tourism: The great patient of coronavirus COVID-2019, MPRA Paper 99666, University Library of Munich, Germany, 2020.

59 Bizzarri C., Ceschin F., L'attrattività turistica dell'Italia nello scenario geopolitico post covid-19, Bozzato S. (a cura di), Geografie del Covid-19, Università di Roma, 2020.

60 Bulin D., Tenie I.P., "Preliminary assessment of the COVID-19 pandemic impact on the tourism industry", *Global Economic Observer*, "Nicolae Titulescu" University of Bucharest, Faculty of Economic Sciences, Vol. 8 No. 1, May 2020, pp. 41–46.

61 Corbisiero F., Monaco S., "Post-pandemic tourism resilience: Changes in Italians' travel behavior and the possible responses of

tourist cities", *Worldwide Hospitality and Tourism Themes*, Vol. 13 No. 3, 2021, pp. 401–417.

62 International Labor Organization (ILO), The impact of COVID-19 on the tourism sector, May 2020.

63 Federazione Italiana del Turismo, Coronavirus: The amount of EUR 200 million for commission for March 2020. Retrieved from: http:// www.assoturismo.it/coronavirus-assoturismo-gia-bruciati-200-milioni-di-euro-di-prenotazioni-per-marzo-messina-lavorare-per-la-normalizzazione-o-salta-tutto.html.

64 ISTAT, Una stagione mancata: impatto del Covid-19 sul turismo, April 2020.

65 Confcommercio.it, Confturismo e Coronavirus [online]. Available at: https://www.confcommercio.it/-/confturismo-coronavirus, 2020.

66 Statista, 2021, Monthly spending of international tourists in Italy from January 2019 to August 2021, Statista research department source link bancaditalia.it.

67 Statista, 2021, Monthly tourism balance in Italy 2019–2021, Statista research department source link bancaditalia.it

68 Camilli M., *"The impact of COVID-19 on Italian tourism. Current scenario, opportunity and future tourism organizational strategies"*, ICBGE 2020 22nd International Conference on Business, Globalization and Economics on November 16–17, 2020 at Jeddah, Saudia Arabia, 2020.

69 Bulin D., Tenie I.P., op. cit.

70 Organisation for Economic Cooperation and Development (OECD), Tourism policy responses to the coronavirus (COVID-19), 2 June 2020.

71 Pasquinelli C., Trunfio M., "The missing link between overtourism and post-pandemic tourism. Framing Twitter debate on the Italian tourism crisis", *Journal of Place Management and Development*, ahead-of-print, 2021.

72 Monaco S., "Turismo in lockdown. Tra misure economiche e politiche simboliche", *Rivista Trimestrale di Scienza dell'amministrazione*, Vol. 2, 2020, pp. 1–18.

73 Chiappa G.D., "COVID-19 pandemic and the accommodation sector in Sardinia, Italy: Impacts and response actions", in Gowreesunkar V.G., Maingi S.W., Roy H., Micera R. (Eds.), *Tourism destination management in a post-pandemic context (tourism security-safety and post conflict destinations)*. Bingley: Emerald Publishing Limited, 2021, pp. 49–65.

74 World Bank, *Rebuilding tourism competitiveness: Tourism response, recovery and resilience to the COVID-19 crisis*. Washington, DC: Markets & Technology Global Tourism Team, July 2020.

75 https://www.mckinsey.com/business-functions/risk/our-insights/covid-19-implications-for-business.

76 Organisation for Economic Cooperation and Development (OECD), Tourism policy responses to the coronavirus (COVID-19), 2 June 2020.

77 World Bank, op. cit.

78 Camilleri M.A., "Strategic dialogic communication through digital media during COVID-19 crisis", in Camilleri M.A. (Ed.), *Strategic*

corporate communication in the digital age. Bingley: Emerald Publishing Limited, 2021, pp. 1–18; Oweis T.I., "The role of social media in promoting citizenship values of international students during the COVID-19 global health crisis", *International Journal of Human Rights in Healthcare,* ahead-of-print, 2021.

79 Tzanelli R., "Post-viral tourismicatinospl's antagonistic tourist imaginaries", *Journal of Tourism Futures,* Vol. 7 No. 3, 2021, pp. 377–389.

80 Dupeyras, A., Haxton, P. and Stacey, J., The Covid-19 crisis and tourism: Response and recovery measures to support the tourism sector in OECD countries. Global Health and Covid-19. Task force 11 COVID-19: Multidisciplinary approaches to complex problems. Vancouver, 2020.

81 Carlisle S., Ivanov S., Dijkmans C., "The digital skills divide: evidence from the European tourism industry", *Journal of Tourism Futures,* ahead-of-print, 2021.

82 Navarro E.J., Ortega P.G., Bernier T.E., *Propuestas de reflexión desde el turismo frente al covid-19 Incertidumbre, impacto y recuperación.* Instituto Universitario de Investigación de Inteligencia e Innovación Turística de la Universidad de Málaga, April 2020.

83 Lama R., Rai A., "Challenges in developing sustainable tourism post COVID-19 pandemic", in Gowreesunkar V.G., Maingi S.W., Roy H., Micera R. (Eds.), *Tourism destination management in a post-pandemic context (tourism security-safety and post conflict destinations).* Bingley: Emerald Publishing Limited, 2021, pp. 233–244; Marques I.C.P., Serrasqueiro Z., Nogueira F., "Covid-19 and organisational development: Important signs of a new pillar for sustainability", *Social Responsibility Journal,* ahead-of-print, 2021.

84 Carbone F., *Tourism destination management post COVID-19 Pandemic: A new humanism for a Human-Centered-Tourism (Tourism 5.0),* School of Marketing and Management & Centre for Trust, Peace, and Social Relations, Coventry University, 2019.

85 Kumar J., Garg A., "Covid-19 vs. overtourism: Challenges or opportunities for tourist destinations: Theoretical perspective", in Sharma A., Hassan A. (Eds.), *Overtourism as destination risk (tourism security-safety and post conflict destinations).* Bingley: Emerald Publishing Limited, 2021, pp. 263–274.

86 Tzu-Ling Chen C., Wickens E., "Tourism industry resilience issues in urban areas during COVID-19", *International Journal of Tourism Cities,* Vol. 7 No. 3, 2021, pp. 861–879.

87 Lew A.A., Cheer J.M., Haywood M., Brouder P., Salazar N.B., "Visions of travel and tourism after the global COVID-19 transformation of 2020", *Tourism Geographies,* Vol. 22 No. 3, 2020, pp. 455–466; Amaro D., "Crisis management and resilient destinations during Covid-19 in the Southern European countries", in Seabra C., Paiva O., Silva C., Abrantes J.L. (Eds.), *Pandemics and travel (tourism security-safety and post conflict destinations).* Bingley: Emerald Publishing Limited, 2021, pp. 243–258.

88 Morvillo A., Becheri E., *Dalla crisi alle opportunità per il futuro del turismo in Italia,* Consiglio Nazionale delle Ricerche (CNR), Istituto di Ricerca su Innovazione e Servizi per lo Sviluppo, Napoli, 2020.

89 Altshuler A., Schmidt J., "Why does resilience matter? Global implications for the tourism industry in the context of COVID-19", *Worldwide Hospitality and Tourism Themes*, Vol. 13 No. 3, 2021, pp. 431–436.

90 Espiner S., Orchiston C., Higham J., "Resilience and sustainability: A
complementary relationship? Towards a practical conceptual model
for the sustainability – Resilience nexus in tourism", *Journal of Sustainable Tourism*, Vol. 25 No. 10, 2017, pp. 1385–1400.

91 Carbone F., op. cit.

92 Taleb Rifai, https://peacetourism.org/rifai/

93 Boons F.A., et al., *Covid-19, changing social practices and the transition to sustainable production and consumption, Version 1.0*. Manches-
ter: Sustainable Consumption Institute, May 2020.

94 Kumar J., Garg A., op. cit.

95 Jones P., Comfort D., "The COVID-19 crisis, tourism and sustainable", *Athens Journal of Tourism*, Vol. 7 No. 2, June 2020, pp. 75–86.

96 Romagosa F., "The COVID-19 crisis: Opportunities for sustainable
and proximity tourism", *Tourism Geographies*, Vol. 22 No.3, 2020, pp.
690–669.

97 Fletcher R., Murray Mas I.M., Blanco-Romero A., Blázquez-Salom
M., "Tourism and degrowth: An emerging agenda for research and
praxis", *Journal of Sustainable Tourism*, Vol. 27 No. 12, 2019, pp.
1745–1763.

98 Cohen A., "Living in a Covid-19 world", *The Milbank Quarterly*, Vol.
98 No. 2, June 2020, pp. 227–234.

99 Romagosa, F., "The COVID-19 crisis: Opportunities for sustainable
and proximity tourism", *Tourism Geographies*, Vol. 22 No. 3, 2020, pp.
690–694.

100 Higgins-Desbiolles F., Carnicelli S., Krolikowski C., Wijesinghe G.,
Boluk K., "Degrowing tourism: Rethinking tourism", *Journal of Sustainable Tourism*, Vol. 27 No. 2, 2019, pp. 1926–1944.

101 The European Commission Science and Knowledge Service,
COVID-19, tourist behavior, jobs and policy options, EU science
HUB, 2020.

102 Seabra C., AlAshry M., Çınar K., Raja I., Reis M., Sadiq N., "Re-
strictions' acceptance and risk perception by young generations in a
COVID-19 context", *International Journal of Tourism Cities*, Vol. 7
No. 2, 2021, pp. 463–491.

103 Dubois L.E., Dimanche F., "The futures of entertainment dependent
cities in a post-COVID world", *Journal of Tourism Futures*, Vol. 7 No.
3, 2021, pp. 364–376.

4 Analysis of Consumer's Attitudes to a Range of Tourism Activities and Destinations in the Light of COVID-19 Crisis

4.1 The empirical data

4.1.1 Effects of COVID-19 on tourism

The initial appearance of COVID-19 and its European spread in 2020 changed the lives of millions of people,[1] causing human suffering and significant loss in Italy and around the world, in particular, in the tourism sector.[2] Although tourism has an incomparable capacity for resilience, unlike previous crises, the world is now facing an unprecedented emergency. The tourism sector has proved to be a very vulnerable sector, subjected to high constraints, that is heavily affected by the unexpected, such as this most recent and sudden crisis.[3] As a result, several challenges have emerged that the tourism industry must address in order to recover. Moreover, because consumers play a central role in the economy, their beliefs and expectations are likely to be crucial for understanding the economy's response to the pandemic.

While consumption is habitual, it is also contextual, and there are four major contexts which govern or disrupt consumer habits.[4] The first is the change in the social context due to life events such as getting married, having children and moving from one city to another; this context also includes workplace, community, neighbours, and friends. The second context is technology; the innovative technologies that emerge are capable of breaking old habits. Sometimes these are technologies that already exist but are used in different sectors. The most important technologies that have evolved in recent years are smartphones, the use of the Internet and e-commerce. All of these have facilitated the possibility of doing research and ordering online easily and quickly. The impact of these technologies on how people shop and on consumer products and services has been huge.

DOI: 10.4324/9781003268963-5

The third context that has a decisive influence on consumer habits are the rules and regulations linked to public and shared spaces. The fourth context is the most difficult to predict and relates to natural disasters, such as hurricanes, earthquakes and pandemics. The COVID-19 pandemic falls in this group. This event disrupted both consumption and production, as well as the supply chain, in an unexpected way.[5]

Not only have consumer habits changed during this period, but some habits have also very likely changed forever. The lockdowns and social distancing required to tackle the COVID-19 virus have caused disruptions and lasting changes in consumer behaviour. In such a context, the crucial questions are as follows: What will be the new travel trends in the post-pandemic era? What potentially new tourism behaviours might emerge? Will consumers need to resort to their own moral judgements when deciding whether, when and how to travel? These questions are especially important for Business to Consumer (B2C) companies, which need to recover from the COVID-19 crisis as soon as possible by finding one or more solutions to their current challenges. Only by discovering the answers to consumers' questions and doubts will these companies be able to build a lasting competitive advantage and create a risk management process as part of their flexible and sustainable business model for the future. Therefore, it is essential for these businesses to understand changes in consumer behaviours as early as possible, even in advance, in order to adapt their business model quickly enough.[6] Companies that succeed in doing this will have assured success, as they will be able to quickly adapt to new consumer behaviours and create a competitive or first-mover advantage in their specific market.[7]

Trends in tourist behaviour can be used to estimate the tourism sector's likely recovery time following the end of the pandemic. Tourist behaviour is the combination of interactions between internal factors (motivation, attitudes, beliefs, etc.) and external factors (economic environment, security, socio-cultural environment, etc.). For travellers, safety is a crucial consumer property; indeed, the perception of risk is of particular importance in the tourist decision-making process. Destinations can only attract visitors if they provide a safe and secure environment in which travellers feel protected from threats during their stay. When consumers are deciding where and when to travel, they will perceive the risks associated with the purchase of the product.[8] The perception of risk factors related to tourism affects consumer behaviour, which, in turn, influences the choice of purchase. Faced with the perception of an external danger, tourists adopt new consumer practices, which has been illustrated in several cases: more trip cancellations, more car trips that prevent intense contact with people, more time spent outdoors, more last-minute reservations, more attention to eco-tourism and more concern for hygiene. Thus, as has been the case after previous crises, new tourist concerns, apprehensions and demands emerge.[9]

Therefore, it is vitally important to predict the trajectory of change in consumer behaviour in the tourism sector so that tourism managers can address the crisis and lay the foundations for a resilience strategy that responds to the situation and provides a means of reflection by identifying changes in tourist behaviour in the aftermath of COVID-19. The change in consumer behaviour and experience based on previous disasters must contribute to the businesses' resilience. Above all, small and medium businesses often have a low propensity to manage risks and to carry out a risk planning process because of a lack of resources, but also, in particular, because of a lack of skills. It is important that companies possess the skills needed to adapt to change, ranging from business planning and adapting business models for increased flexibility to changing their risk management process. Even in the post-pandemic future, tourism business managers must ensure that risk planning remains a priority.

4.1.2 Long-term COVID-19 effects: the hypotheses

It is important for tourism businesses to understand tourist behaviour in order to drive their development. This includes the choice of tourist destinations, the evaluation of tourist destinations, and the intentions of future tourist behaviour. Although it is extremely difficult to predict the behaviour of tourists after a crisis, an empirical study was conducted to learn about the sensitivity of tourists faced with a health crisis such as that of COVID-19. The aim was to discover what changes in consumption travellers had made as a consequence of the pandemic. Understanding fluctuating tourist behaviour guides strategies and actions to provide timely and adequate responses to support the recovery of the tourism industry. The findings of this research provide a basis for reflection for tourism enterprises and managers seeking to recover from this complicated situation. The study offers important insights into the short- and long-term effects of COVID-19 on tourist behaviour in Italy and identifies significant shifts in consumer preferences related to travel because of the pandemic.

We decided to analyse Italy because the Italian population represents an important reference for the tourism sector since many Italians go on vacation habitually. The following are the summary data for the pre-pandemic year 2019, according to the National Institute of Statistics.[10] In 2019, overnight trips made by residents in Italy were 71 million and 883,000. Holiday trips accounted for about 89% of the total, while work trips constituted about 11%. Holidays were the reason for 93.4% of overnight stays (6.6% were for business trips), while 49% of trips and 79.6% of nights spent on the road were considered "long" holidays (four or more nights). In the summer, 37.8% of the population (which currently amounts to about 60 million inhabitants) takes at least one vacation.

One of the objectives of this work is to predict changes in tourism behaviour that might occur among Italian consumers after the COVID-19 health crisis, in particular changes related to the choice of destination or the organizational aspects of travel. This study relies on the assumption that, due to the change in economic conditions and regulations during the crisis, consumers must make significant changes in their choice of holiday destination. The hypotheses of this research are established based on concerns that tourists expressed on social media networks about their general perception of travelling after COVID-19. Thus, after the COVID-19 crisis, when tourists plan their next trip, we propose that:

HP1: Tourists will prefer destinations close to their hometowns.

HP2: Tourists will avoid known and expensive destinations, preferring less-known destinations with fewer tourists.

HP3: Tourists will pay more attention to the sanitary standards of the host destinations (hygiene, cleanliness, etc.) and will be more interested in the quality of health care than they were before the pandemic.

HP4: Tourists' psychological factors will affect their vacation choices (fear, anxiety, loneliness, etc.).

These hypotheses were tested through a survey and descriptive statistical analysis of the data.

The second objective of the study was to analyse and predict Italian tourists' intentions regarding changes in the sharing economy sector, with a focus on accommodation. In the last few years, the sharing economy has had a strong diffusion and has involved many business sectors ranging from home sharing (like Airbnb) to shared mobility (Blablacar and Uber).[11] Mobility sharing became available for all types of demands ranging from micro-mobility (bikes and scooters) and medium distance (ride hailing) to long-distance offerings (e.g., car sharing). These services have grown rapidly, but other sharing services, such as home services, co-working spaces or peer-to-peer lending, have also become very popular. Before COVID-19, it seemed that everything could be shared, and the industry was growing rapidly. However, the sharing economy has suffered significantly during the COVID-19 crisis due to changes in consumer behaviour. Restrictions on people's mobility due to the increased risk of infection have led to a reduction in the use of sharing services. Furthermore, the interruption of services and the forced limitation of socially shared spaces have heavily marked the sharing economy and created new concerns for the safety of users of sharing services. Because of the perceived higher risk of infections in shared spaces, the second objective of the study is to ascertain whether or not there will be a notable decline in the demand for sharing economy services after the COVID-19 crisis. To test this hypothesis, the research identifies the social determinants impacting tourists' decisions before and after COVID-19.

4.1.3 The two questionnaires

The research is a descriptive study administered using an online questionnaire (Google Formular) as a survey tool. Questionnaires were sent via the Internet (social media and e-mail). This choice made it possible to survey a large number of people while covering a wide geographical area. The number of respondents for the first questionnaire was 2,539, of which, only the 2,488 Italian residents were taken into account for the purposes of this research. The second questionnaire had 1,421 respondents, of which 1,408 were Italian residents. Data were collected during two different periods of time: the first questionnaire was launched between the end of September and the middle of October 2020, right after the end of summer vacations, while the second questionnaire was launched between the end of September and the end of October 2021. Individual respondents were anonymized to ensure confidentiality. Participants revealed insights about their behaviour and gave indications regarding their choices and intended behaviour after the crisis has ended. Additionally, the survey provides detailed behavioural insights regarding different demographic levels (age, gender, etc.).

The purpose of the first questionnaire is to identify the impact of COVID-19 on tourist behaviour, in particular the impact it had on travellers' choices and decisions (such as their choice of destinations, the aspects involved in organizing a holiday trip, etc.). The purpose of the second questionnaire is to identify the impact of COVID-19 on tourist behaviour in comparison to the results of the first survey and take into account new situational factors, such as vaccination availability and status and Green Pass. The questionnaires are divided into three main sections.

The first section asks circumstantial questions that make it possible to identify the sociological profile of the respondents (age, gender, profession, location, marital status, and the number of children). The second section aims to identify possible changes in tourist behaviour regarding the respondents' choice of holiday destination and the reasons that pushed them to make the particular decisions that they made. Respondents in this section are also asked to rate the level of importance of some specific factors that contributed to their decision-making process regarding tourist destinations, both before and after the COVID-19 pandemic. Some of the specific factors that affect the choice to go on vacation are insecurity about travelling abroad, disposable income, fear of becoming infected, fear of quarantine, desire to return to normal life, destinations with fewer tourists, destinations less affected by COVID-19, destinations characterized by a good health care system, and personal reasons. In addition to these factors, the second questionnaire, carried out in 2021, adds four new variables such as the vaccination, Green Pass, more control thanks to swabs and greater safety. Respondents are also asked to rate the level of importance of each factor (cleanliness/hygiene, disposable income, less crowed places, proximity to the hometown, importance of all-inclusive option, general services like swimming pool, parking, gym, etc.) at the moment when they are choosing their vacation destination. Finally, the third section asks questions about accommodations via the sharing economy and, specifically, about how their use of such accommodations changed during the pandemic. Respondents are required to explain why they did or did not choose to use an accommodation sharing platform and to clarify if they will or will not be willing to share after the COVID-19 pandemic.

4.2 Data analysis of results of 2020

Given the pre-existing available data, it was possible to carry out a limited number of descriptive analyses in terms of frequencies and percentages through the use of Microsoft Excel. Graphics and tables were created to analyse the available data and to understand the relationships and the main differences between variables. The results obtained will be presented here, starting with the information related to survey respondents' profiles and general data. Successively, data and evidence about the availability to travel and destination preferences will be described, with the support of charts realized by filtering data according to age range. Ultimately, respondents' perceptions regarding sharing economy topics will be evaluated.

4.2.1 Profile of survey respondents

In this study, questionnaires were distributed via Google forms and sent via the Internet (social media and e-mail). The total number of respondents was 2,539 people, of which, for the purpose of this study, only the 2,488 Italian residents are taken into account. The majority of respondents were women (73%). The respondents were divided into five main categories based on age in order to better understand the differences between preferences according to age range (maturity, adulthood, elderliness, etc.). The majority of respondents were millennials with 63% being 18–24 and 9% 25–30. Next, 12% were 31–40 years old, 9% were 41–50, and 7% were over 50 years old (Figure 4.1).

As we can observe, respondents are dominated by millennials, which is the generation of people born between 1981 and 2000.[12] The millennial generation actively uses the Internet, which is probably

Age range of respondents

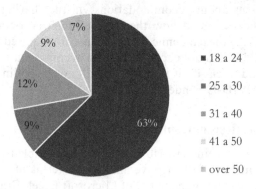

Figure 4.1 Age range of respondents

why they are the dominant respondent group, since completing the online survey is very simple and accessible. In terms of marital status, 46% of the respondents were unmarried, while the remaining percentage is dominated by engaged and married respondents (25% and 20%, respectively), and there is a very low percentage of cohabitee (8%) and divorced (1%). Most of the respondents were students (63%), while 31% were workers, and 2% were students/workers. These data confirm the fact that the majority of the respondents were young people, mostly students or working students. A small percentage, 3% and 1%, respectively, were unemployed or pensioners.

4.2.2 Availability to travel

This first part of the survey aims to demonstrate the assumption that changes in economic conditions and regulations during the crisis forced consumers to make significant changes regarding their holiday choices, both with regard to the destination and the reasons that influenced their choice. During the lockdown period, there was no possibility to travel, but afterward, people started to go on vacation. Indeed, the survey shows that 74% had taken a holiday in Italy between the months of July and September, despite the fact that the majority of them didn't reserve any kind of trip before COVID-19 (56%). Only 15% indicated that they did not travel during the pandemic (Figure 4.2).

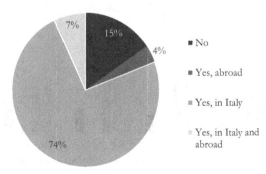

Figure 4.2 Travel June–September

These data, as the graph visualizes, show how strong the desire was to return to normal life and to start travelling again, after the lockdown period, and how this factor was much more important than any fear of contracting the virus.

4.2.3 Consumer destination choice: to travel or not

Now, the focus of the research will be on analysing the factors that influenced consumers when choosing their travel destinations, both for those who travelled and for those who chose not to due to COVID-19. Respondents who travelled highlighted the insecurity of travelling abroad, confirmed by the fact that only 4% decided to travel outside Italy.

The analysis of these variables has taken into account the different age ranges of respondents, which, in some cases, led to distinctive and noteworthy answers. St0arting from the most selected factor for every single age range, the majority of respondents who travelled selected the desire to return to normal life as the main reason (Figure 4.3).

It is interesting to observe how much the desire to return to normal life rose above all other factors, in particular the fear of contracting the virus and having to quarantine. To be specific, the fear of the virus was moderately important for respondents in all age ranges, with percentages between 35% and 39% among millennials, 31%–34% for people in the 31–50-year-old range, and 43% (the highest) for respondents over 50 (Figure 4.4).

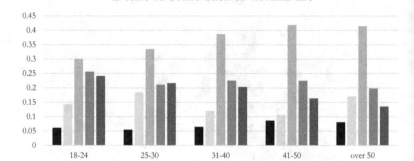

Figure 4.3 Desire to return to "normal life"

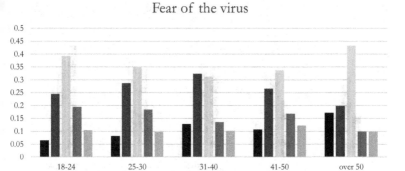

Figure 4.4 Fear of the virus

When considering the fear of having to quarantine as a factor that affected their holiday plans, the 31–40-year-olds and the 41–50-year-olds showed the most concern, with 17% and 19%, respectively, rating this factor as "very important", in contrast to the small percentage of respondents between 18 and 24 years old and over 50 years old, for whom 13% and 7%, respectively rated it as "very important". This difference in importance is noteworthy because it is probably related to the fact that people from 31–50 years old belong to the working category. Thus, it is likely that the fear of being forced to stay at home is related to the fear of significant repercussions at work, and people just want to avoid the risk of not being able to return to work.

When considering disposable income as a factor in their choice of holiday destination (Figure 4.5), the majority of individuals rated it as "unimportant" or "slightly important". Very few respondents over the age of 50 (2%) took this factor into account, while the percentages who cared increased to 15% and 12% for millennials. Only 14% of respondents between the ages of 18–24 said that disposable income was "unimportant". As age increased so did the number of respondents who were not impacted by disposable income as a factor. This difference is likely due to the fact that individuals who are 31 and older have regular jobs and more economic stability than younger people. Nevertheless, this factor offers an interesting point of comparison, since it is expected that people will find this factor to be important after the pandemic crisis has abated.

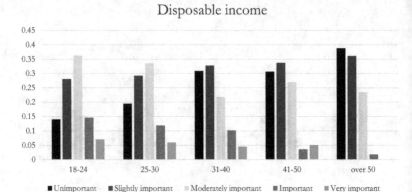

Figure 4.5 Disposable income

According to the remaining factors, data show that respondents preferred destinations that were less affected by COVID-19, with no difference in percentages between all age ranges. In particular, they tended to prefer less crowded destinations, although this factor was impacted by age. Only 32% of young people gave importance to this factor, while 50% of respondents over age 50 considered it be moderately important to select less crowded destinations.

For respondents who decided not to go on vacation in 2020, the two most influential factors were fear of the virus and fear of quarantine. These, surprisingly, ranked higher than lack of disposable income. The majority of respondents (30%–46% depending on age range) rated their fear of quarantine as "moderately important", while 15%–22% (again, depending on age range) ranked it as "important". In addition, the majority of respondents (31% and 44% depending on age range) rated their fear of the virus as "moderately important", or 13%–28% (again, depending on age range) ranked it as "important".

As previously pointed out, the lack of disposable income was not a determining factor in whether or not respondents chose to go on vacation. Nevertheless, even though this factor was not generally relevant, analysing it by different age ranges provides noteworthy findings. Only 8% of individuals in the 18–24-year-old range rated the lack of disposable income as "unimportant", in contrast to those in the 41–50 range, of whom 41% rated this factor as "unimportant" and the over 50 range, of whom 50% rated this factor as "unimportant". To further highlight the relevance to this factor,

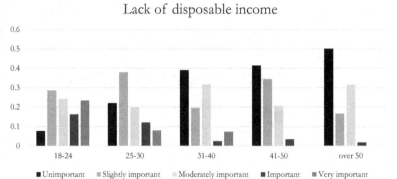

Lack of disposable income

Figure 4.6 Lack of disposable income

0% of respondents between 41 and 50 years old rated this factor as "very important", while 23% of young people did consider lack of disposable income to be "very important" (Figure 4.6). These numbers once again underline that younger respondents, especially between 18 and 24 years of age, are more concerned about the economic aspect than older people.

The last factor, which is not particularly relevant for the study, is the lack of possibility to take time off work, which the majority of young respondents (50% and 56%) rated as "unimportant", followed by 56% for the age range 31–40, 59% between 41 and 50 years old and finally 70% for people with more than 50 years old. This factor is highly correlated with the fact that a high percentage of respondents selected two or more weeks as their desired travel time, meaning that they prefer to have significant time available for vacation.

4.2.4 *Place and holiday duration*

The research then gives further information related to the selection of time and place of holiday plans. Results show that most respondents' (46%) desired travel time is two or more weeks, while 34% opted for one week; a small percentage (4%–16%) stated a couple of days or weekends. These data show that consumers are willing to spend a lot of time on vacation despite the crisis and the impact of the pandemic. In terms of place selection, the dominant choice (60%) was seaside resorts, followed by natural places/mountains

Holiday Location

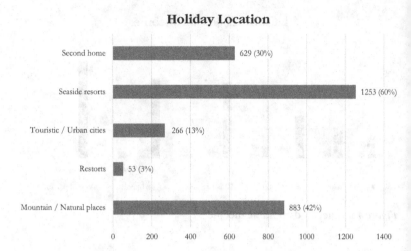

Figure 4.7 Holiday location

(42%), while only 3% and 13% preferred tourist cities and resorts (Figure 4.7). It is worth highlighting that 30% of respondents took advantage of second homes or friend's homes as places to spend their summer vacation, possibly to avoid crowded destinations, or because of fear of contracting the virus.

4.2.5 Factors taken into account when deciding on a holiday destination: comparison between pre- and post-COVID-19 responses (referring to 2020)

This part of the study discusses how the importance of some factors regarding holiday destination choices changed before and after COVID-19 and identifies the main discrepancies and changes in behaviour. In this part of the study, we did not divide respondents according to age range due to the fact that the percentages of the responses did not vary among the age ranges. Among the various factors, only the most relevant are taken into account, according to the aspects where difference is consistent. Therefore, disposable income, the all-inclusive option, and secondary services were not considered relevant for the research, since the differences between percentages from the pre- and post-COVID-19 responses were roughly identical.

Cleanliness / Hygiene

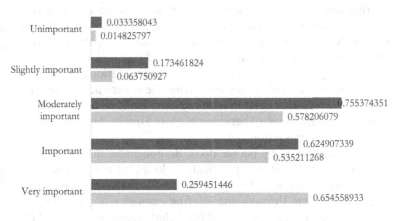

Figure 4.8 Cleanliness/hygiene, pre- and post-COVID-19 comparison

The factor for which responses shifted the most between the two surveys was cleanliness/hygiene, which 26% of respondents (350 total) rated as "very important" before the pandemic, but 65% (883 total) rated it as very important after the pandemic (Figure 4.8).

Another important factor that completely changed after COVID-19 was individuals' preference for less crowded destinations. Before the pandemic, 19% of respondents identified this factor as "unimportant", while after the outbreak of the virus, only 3% continued to identify this factor as "unimportant", On the other hand, there was a complete shift—from 5% before COVID-19 to 21% after COVID-19—among respondents who find it "very important" to select less crowded destinations. Last but not least was the issue of proximity to their hometown, a factor which was taken into account when deciding on a holiday destination. Before COVID-19, approximately 85% of respondents considered choosing the nearest destinations "unimportant" (43%) or only "slightly important" (42%). After COVID-19, 29% considered this factor to be "moderately important", whereas previously only 10% had considered it so. Finally, there was an 8% increase in the number of individuals who considered this factor to be important.

4.2.6 *Tourism and the sharing economy*

The last part of the survey was designed to collect information about Italian tourists' changing intentions regarding the sharing economy sector, with a focus on accommodation. The section was carried out to evaluate the assumption that due to the increased risk of infection through sharing services and the implementation of mobility restrictions, consumers demanded fewer services from the sharing economy during the COVID-19 crisis. In terms of survey data regarding sharing economy accommodations, the majority of respondents (61%) had never tried the experience, while 39% had. These results suggest that a large number of respondents were unaware of this kind of service or, more simply, preferred other types of accommodation.

To demonstrate why people do or do not prefer this type of accommodation, the study specifically asks about the respondents' motives for this choice. The main motive for those who have made accommodations through the sharing economy is an economic concern (60%); the majority thinks that accommodation sharing platforms offer much more affordable accommodations. It is, therefore, interesting that this factor alone did not affect most people's decisions. Indeed, 44% of respondents selected the option "I wasn't alone but with other friends" as their second main motive. Respondents gave little importance (33%) to the availability and

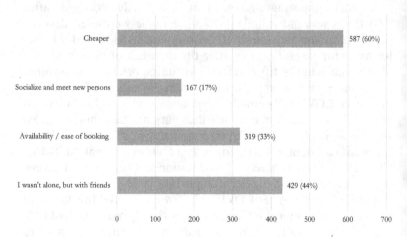

Figure 4.9 Reasons for using accommodation sharing platforms

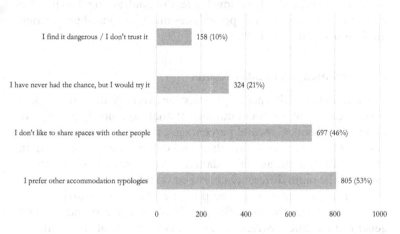

I find it dangerous / I don't trust it — 158 (10%)

I have never had the chance, but I would try it — 324 (21%)

I don't like to share spaces with other people — 697 (46%)

I prefer other accommodation typologies — 805 (53%)

0   200   400   600   800   1000

Figure 4.10 Reasons for not using accommodation sharing platforms

ease of booking and even less (17%) to socializing and meeting new people (Figure 4.9).

The main reasons that some people chose not to use accommodation sharing platforms are their preference for other types of accommodation (53%) and because sharing spaces with other people was not a valuable option for them (46%). In addition, 21% of respondents said they would like to try such accommodations but have never had the chance, while a small percentage (10%) find it dangerous (Figure 4.10).

Following the general analysis, we turn our attention to the changes in individuals' willingness to seize the opportunities offered by share accommodation platforms in light of the post-COVID-19 situation. Confirming the initial hypothesis, the number of individuals who said they would not use this type of service (74%) increased and the number of people who said they would continue to use it (26%) decreased. Of those who said they would continue to use accommodation sharing platforms, 75% said that their primary reason for doing so was economic convenience. None of them were influenced by the desire to socialize or a lack of fear of the virus. Of those respondents who reported that they would not use accommodation sharing platforms after COVID-19, 51% said their primary reason was a preference for other types of accommodations, while 43% said their primary reason was a fear of becoming infected with the virus. These data show how the fear of contracting the virus led consumers to change their preferences and opinions about accommodation sharing platforms.

4.3 Data analysis of 2021 results

Considering the existence of pre-existing available data, it was possible to carry out a limited number of analyses, mostly descriptive in terms of frequencies and percentages, through the use of the applicant Microsoft Excel. Graphics and tables have been created, in order to analyse the available data and to understand the relationship and the main differences between variables.

The results obtained will be presented hereafter, starting from the information related to the profile of survey respondents and general data. Successively data and evidence about the availability to travel and destination preferences will be described, with the creation of charts realized by filtering data according to age range. Afterwards, the perception of respondents regarding Sharing Economy's topics will be evaluated. Ultimately, the results of the two questionnaries will be compared to analyse and understand the changes between the two years.

4.3.1 Profile of survey respondents

For this study, questionnaires were created using Google forms and distributed via the Internet (social media and e-mail). There were 1,421 respondents, of which, for the purposes of the research, 1,408 Italian residents were considered. In general, it's possible to say that the profile of the 2021 survey respondents matches that of the 2020 respondents, but analysing it in detail provides a more nuanced understanding. For the 2021 survey, 69% of the respondents were women. Moreover, as with the 2020 survey results, we divided the respondents into five main categories according to age in order to better understand the different preferences according to age range (maturity, adulthood, elderliness, etc.).

Of the total number of respondents, 82% were aged 18–24, 10% were aged 25–30, 3% were aged 31–40, 3% were aged 41–50, and 2% were over 50 years old.

As in the first research questionnaire, the millennial generation (those born between 1981 and 2000) was the dominant responding generation. In terms of marital status, 57% of respondents were unmarried, 34% were engaged, 4% were married, 4% were

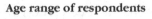

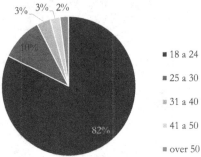

Figure 4.11 Age range of respondents

cohabitating, and 1% were divorced. Most (84%) of the respondents were students, 11% were workers, and a small percentage were students/workers. These data are sensible given that the majority of the respondents were young people, mostly students or working students. A small percentage were unemployed or pensioners.

4.3.2 *Availability to travel*

This first part of the survey aimed to demonstrate the assumption that consumers are expected to make changes regarding their holiday choices with regard to both destinations and the reasons for their choices. Thus, this section of the survey asked respondents about any changes in their willingness to go on vacation in the past year. According to the results, 70% of the respondents went on holiday in Italy between the months of July and September, while only 12% said they would not go. These data, as the graph shows, signal how strong the desire to still travel remains and how this factor is much more important than fear of contracting the virus.

4.3.3 *Factors that influenced the choice to travel compared to 2020*

This section focused on the factors that influenced choices regarding destination for those consumers who did travel in 2021, as compared to the previous year, 2020. Here, new variables were analysed. Based on our findings, the introduction of security measures,

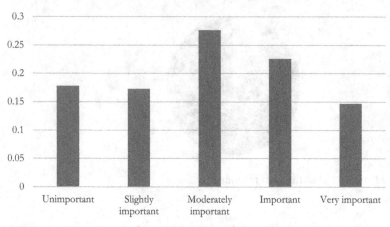

Figure 4.12 Vaccination and Green Pass

such as vaccinations, the Green Pass, and swabs, increased consumers' feelings of safety and security when deciding to travel and overcame their fear of the virus. In particular, fear of the virus decreased considerably: 35% of respondents considered this variable to be "slightly important", and only 7% considered it to be "very important".

This result shows that the introduction of new security measures made people feel more comfortable and safer in regards to travel, alleviating their fear of the virus. Indeed, most respondents identified the variable related to vaccinations and the Green Pass (Figure 4.12) as "moderately important" or "important".

As a result of these data in Figure 4.13, it is possible to say that people felt safer about travelling 2021 than they did in 2020.

Next, 30% of respondents rated the variable related to swabs as "moderately important", while 26% felt that it was "slightly important", and 20% said it was "unimportant". The close percentages here are noteworthy, as we expected the number respondents who felt safer thanks to swabs to be higher. This finding is probably due to the fact that a lot of people still feel insecure and do not believe that swabs are a reliable enough measure to make them feel more comfortable and safer.

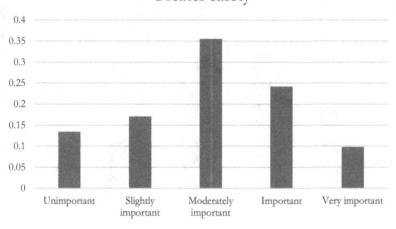

Figure 4.13 Greater safety

4.3.4 Consumer destination: choice to travel or not

Now, we turn on our attention to the factors that influenced travel choices both for those who travelled and for those who did not, as in the first questionnaire. Respondents who travelled noted that the insecurity of travelling abroad was an important factor in their decision to stay in the country; only 4% decided to travel outside Italy. The analysis of these variables does not consider age range differences because most of them belonged to the same age range.

Most respondents who travelled selected the desire to return to normal life as the main reason influencing their decision to do so. Indeed, the data show how much the desire to return to normal life overcame other factors, in particular the fear of contracting the virus. To be specific, 34% rated the fear of the virus as "slightly important", but just 7% rated it "very important". This is interesting to observe, since it means that a high number of respondents no longer fear the virus (Figure 4.14).

The majority of individuals rated the disposable income factor as "slightly important" or "moderately important", showing that economic considerations were not particularly relevant for their choices. Moreover, according to the remaining factors, the data show that respondents prefer less crowded destinations; 57% rated this factor as "slightly and moderately important" (Figure 4.15).

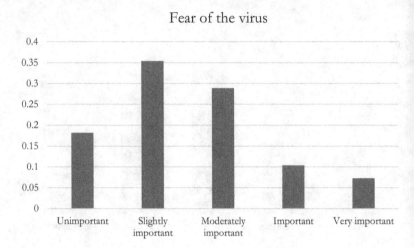

Figure 4.14 Fear of the virus

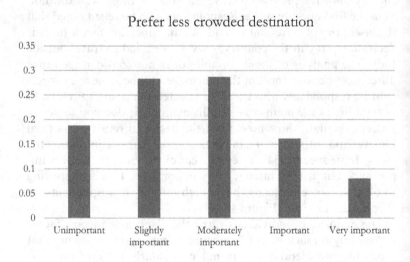

Figure 4.15 Prefer less crowded destinations

It's interesting to observe that respondents who decided not to go on vacation don't give importance to the fear of the virus, fear of quarantine, followed by a lack of disposable income, when deciding not to go on vacation. As a matter of fact, the percentages are similar, respectively, 31%, 29% and 24% as unimportant. The primary factor influencing their decision was personal reasons.

The last factor, which is not particularly relevant for this study, is the lack of holiday, which the majority of respondents evaluated as "unimportant". This factor is highly correlated with the fact that a high percentage of respondents selected two or more weeks as their desired travel time, meaning that they have a significant amount of time available for vacation.

4.3.5 *Place and holiday duration*

The study provides further information related to the selection of time and place of tourist destinations. The results show that the majority of respondents (51%) preferred two or more weeks, 35% opted for one week, while a small percentage (10% and 4%, respectively) noted a couple of days or some weekends. These data show that consumers are willing to spend a lot of time on vacation despite the crisis and the impact of the pandemic.

In terms of selecting a place to vacation, most respondents (43%) preferred seaside resorts (43%), followed by natural places/mountain (19%), and touristic cities and second homes (18%), while only 3% preferred resorts. It is noteworthy that compared to previous year, the preference for tourist sites is much higher, maybe because people feel safer and more comfortable thanks to the new safety measures.

4.4 The comparison of factors taken into account to decide holiday destination between pre- and post-COVID-19 scenarios

This part of the study will discuss how some factors that influence consumers' holiday choices were different before and after COVID-19. Moreover, it will identify the main discrepancies and changes in behaviour. In this part of the findings, the respondents were not divided into age ranges, due to the fact that percentages across them match, and they do not vary according to age.

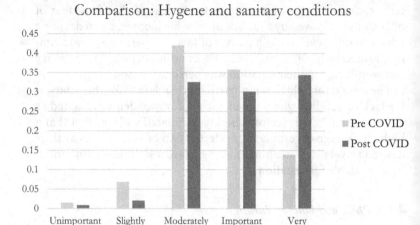

Figure 4.16 Comparison of hygiene and sanitary conditions

Among the various factors, only the most relevant are taken into account, according to the aspects where the difference is consistent. As a matter of fact, disposable income, proximity to hometown, an all-inclusive option, and the importance of secondary services were not considered relevant for the research, since the differences in percentages between before and after COVID-19 are roughly identical. The factor that respondents deemed to be most important in choosing a destination before COVID-19 was cleanliness/hygiene, which 14% ranked as very important). After one year of COVID-19, that percentage increased to 34% (Figure 4.16).

A second important factor that changed after COVID-19 is individuals' preference for less crowded destinations (Figure 4.17). Before the pandemic, 19% of respondents found that factor to be unimportant, but after the outbreak of the virus, that percentage decreased to 2%. On the other hand, those who found it important preferred a less crowded destination changed from 4% before COVID-19 to 19% after COVID-19.

The last part of the survey gathers information regarding changes in Italian tourists' intentions to engage in the sharing economy sector, with a focus on accommodation sharing platforms. The study

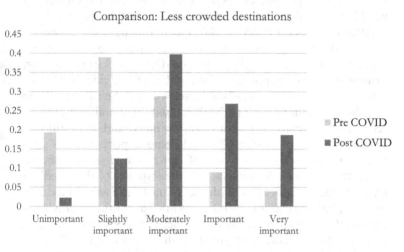

Figure 4.17 Comparison of less crowded destinations

assumed that due to the increased risk of infection from sharing services and the implementation of mobility restrictions, consumers would demand fewer services from the sharing economy during the COVID-19 crisis.

Most respondents (71%) had never used an accommodation sharing platform before the pandemic, while only 29% had. These results suggest that a large number of respondents were unaware of this kind of service or, more simply, preferred other types of accommodation. To determine why people do or do not prefer this type of accommodation, the study specifically asks about the motives behind their choice. The main motive for those who have used accommodation sharing platforms is the economic concern (39%) since the majority think that accommodation sharing platforms are much more affordable than other options. However, 29% of respondents selected the option "I wasn't alone but with other friends", as their second main motive. Little importance was given to the availability and ease of booking (21%) and even less to socializing and meeting new people (11%). As regards individuals who had not tried accommodations sharing platforms, their main reasons were a preference for other types of accommodation (41%) and because sharing spaces with other people was not a valuable option for them

(35%). Sixteen percent of respondents never had the chance but would try it, and a small percentage (8%) finds it dangerous.

After the general analysis, the research focused on changes in individuals' willingness to seize the opportunity to share accommodation platforms in light of the post-COVID-19 situation. Confirming the initial hypothesis, the number of individuals who will not use this type of service (74%) increased, and the number of people who still want to use it (26%) decreased. Economic convenience remains the primary factor for those few individuals who still want to use this type of service (75%), while no importance was given to a desire to socialize or a lack of fear of the virus. In contrast, however, the most relevant aspect is the response of those individuals (the large majority) who do not want to use accommodation sharing platforms after COVID-19. While 36% of those individuals indicated that their preference for other types of accommodation is the most important determinant of their decision, for 31% of respondents, fear of contracting the virus is the most impactful factor. These data show how fear of contracting the virus has changed consumers' preferences for and opinions about accommodation sharing platforms.

4.5 Discussion of the results: comparing 2020 and 2021

In general, it is possible to affirm that the hypothesis of the research, related to the richness of the pre-existing material, has been confirmed by the attained results. More particularly, it's possible to draw many ideas and opportunities from the various outcomes. If we consider changes in tourists' travel intentions and behaviour, the study shows that the behaviour of tourists after the pandemic has new and interesting characteristics. The analysis reveals important changes in consumer preferences, suggesting emerging preferences and alternative tourist opportunities in both 2020 and 2021.

4.5.1 Choosing a nearby destination

The first hypothesis proposed that in the future tourists will prefer destinations closer to their region of residence. Based on our findings, this hypothesis seems to be true in general, but there is a difference between the two years studied. This difference suggests that the COVID-19 pandemic had an impact on people's desire to travel away from home and explore across borders. Specifically, fear of contracting the virus and having to quarantine overcame the desire to travel farther distances. In general, the pandemic does not appear to be creating a negative impact on travel overall, since tourists remain willing to go on holiday and the desire to explore remains high. Nevertheless, people may still be a little more cautious and attentive to the recovery. The desire to return to normal life and, therefore, to travel, is the most relevant data resulting from the research study. It turns out to be the prime reason as many respondents felt the need to go on holiday during the months between June and September of 2020 and 2021.

4.5.2 Choosing an economic and less-known destination with fewer tourists

As for the second hypothesis, many respondents agreed that they wanted a less crowded destination with fewer tourists for their next trip. There is a small percentage difference between 2020 and 2021 (Figure 4.18): the percentage of respondents who are willing to choose a less crowded destination is a little bit lower in 2021 than in 2020. This is because people feel that long-distance journeys are safer, and they can envision a future in which they could go abroad again without any fear of being infected.

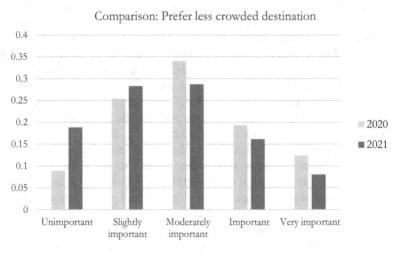

Figure 4.18 Comparison: preference for less crowded destinations

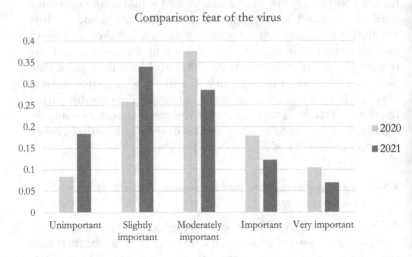

Figure 4.19 Comparison: fear of virus

The significant difference in the number of people who were afraid of contracting the virus between 2020 and 2021 is noteworthy (Figure 4.19). It can be deduced that the importance of this fact in 2020 was related to a combination of personal motivations, such as anxiety and fear regarding the virus.

Security measures, such as vaccinations, the Green Pass, and more control thanks to swabs are most likely responsible for the changes regarding this factor. As the results show, travelling to less crowded places may be the new trend. This desire to be away from the crowds and visit atypical destinations could be an opportunity for new destinations to emerge. Indeed, managers could use this condition to promote their locations and create an original and atypical destination image. This condition can also be interpreted as a desire on the part of tourists to break with the practices of mass tourism. Cities affected by over-tourism should, therefore, adapt to the new requirements by rethinking their economic model, moving towards a softer economy and putting an end to mass tourism by considering alternative and more sustainable measures. Ultimately, it is clear how consumer preferences have shifted prominently from mass tourism towards less crowded tourist destinations, in particular, rural and natural tourism.

These findings for this factor are noteworthy because it was expected that the economic crisis caused by COVID-19 would impact

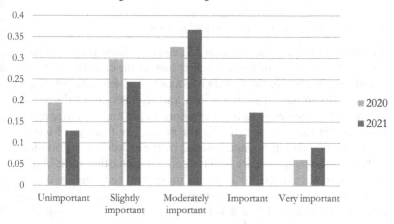

Figure 4.20 Comparison: disposable income

people's disposable income and that, therefore, one of the reasons for not travelling would be a lack of disposable income (Figure 4.20). On the contrary, respondents did not give any importance to this factor, which suggests that, despite the crisis, people's willingness to travel remains quite strong and visible: tourists neither decreased their travel expenses by targeting more affordable destinations nor did they shorten the length of their stay. This behaviour after a financial crisis is quite unusual; it is probably due to the strong desire to return to normal life, to socialize and to feel normal again after the periods of lockdown.

4.5.3 Sanitary conditions and quality of healthcare at the destination

The COVID-19 pandemic has placed hygiene and quality of public healthcare in very important positions. According to the results of the survey, it is clear that one of the major factors that changed in response to COVID-19 is consumers' level of concern and awareness of sanitary conditions and hygiene standards. This indicates that individuals are more concerned with the cleanliness of public spaces, such as hotels, restaurants, and tourist attractions, but they are also more aware of the conditions of access and the quality of the care offered at vacation destinations. Therefore, health standards and the performance of the host destination's health system have become factors that strongly influence the travel decision.

4.5.4 The influence of psychological factors

Another interesting element that has emerged from the research is the strong influence of psychological factors on consumers' travel decisions. Of course, the feeling of anxiety and fear caused by the coronavirus impact their intentions and feelings about the safety of travel, but the desire to return to normal life and socialize again transcended the fear of catching the virus. The feelings of loneliness, isolation and annoyance caused by the lockdown period seem to have made people desire to have contact with other individuals, to return to normal life, to leave the house and see friends and family again. This study reveals the undoubted relevance of psychological factors, which played a key role in tourists' decision-making processes regarding destinations and all other factors related to travel.

The findings of this study clearly demonstrate that consumers' preferences for the accommodations sharing platforms will decrease significantly after the COVID-19 pandemic, and we can expect it to remain this way for a long time. Even before COVID-19, the percentage of respondents using these platforms was not very high, but among respondents who did use this type of accommodation, their main reason was to share costs, underlining the importance of economic convenience. However, after the pandemic, there will be a clear shift towards consumers preferring individual accommodations, and there will be a reduction in sharing accommodations. Overall, the sharing economy industry will be one of the most affected in the whole economy due to the conditions on which this sector is based. Even after the lockdown phase, consumers fear the higher risk of infection that they associate with the sharing economy, and the decreased demand in sharing offerings will put all sharing business models at risk.

4.6 Conclusion: limitations and future recommendations

This research provides important insights about the effects of COVID-19 on tourist consumption behaviour in Italy and identifies significant shifts caused by the pandemic outbreak, analysing the differences between 2020 and 2021. This work aimed to provide an exploratory overview of the changing behaviour of tourists in a society at risk. Moreover, the research helps to quantify shifts in the sharing economy sector based on representative data, thus indicating future consumer intentions. In general, the results indicate that the current COVID-19 pandemic is expected to have an impact on tourists' intentions, which will impact their behaviour in terms of personal safety, economic expenditure, confidence and attitude. In particular, it is noteworthy that all research hypotheses have been confirmed. Tourists do prefer destinations close to their hometowns (Hp_1). They avoid known and expensive destinations (Hp_2). They pay more attention to sanitary standards than they did before the pandemic (Hp_3). Finally, psychological factors do affect their vacation choices (Hp_4). Therefore, stakeholders in the tourism industry need to be resilient, adapt to these shifts in consumption, fulfill tourists' needs by developing lasting competitive advantages, and consider how to overcome the alarming predictions. This will allow firms to manage the crisis successfully and profit from current and future developments.

It can be concluded that COVID-19 will influence travel habits in the future. People will avoid overcrowded destinations and prefer nearby destinations. The pandemic has also drawn attention to issues of hygiene, cleanliness and health conditions in host destinations, which will become significant factors in future travel decisions. Consequently, faced with an anxious clientele, tourism businesses (accommodation, catering, tourist attraction facilities, etc.) should further improve their hygiene conditions to regain consumer confidence and send reassuring messages to their visitors, who attach great importance to safety measures and hygiene standards. Similarly, we also recommend that tourism managers focus on a media strategy, cultivate positive images, and stimulate tourism during and after the COVID-19 crisis.

At the conclusion of this study, it is possible to identify several limitations. First, in terms of sample representation, the number of respondents was quite extensive and not limited by the area of origin, as the majority of respondents is from northern Italy. Moreover, the majority of individuals who participated in the study are millennials, whose characteristics, needs and ways of thinking completely differ from older generations. Therefore, to understand the differences between the place of origin and ages, it would be necessary to analyse a more accurate and well-balanced sample. Thus, for future research, studying the behaviour of each segment independently will allow managers to act according to expectations more specifically (based on, for example, age, gender, place of origin, etc.). The context of future studies may reveal other behaviours that did not emerge during the course of this study. The second aspect regards the fact that there is always a gap between intentions and actual behaviour; thus, it is essential to conduct future research on consumer psychology to understand and, more specifically, to predict the directionality of changing behaviour. In addition, future research will provide a more comprehensive understanding of the influence of the crisis on travel intentions (identified) and actual behaviour (that does occur). As forecasts become more accurate and better defined and understood, recovery strategies can be better controlled and targeted to ensure maximum effectiveness.

Finally, it should be specified that the analysis carried out on the collected data and the hypotheses defined were evaluated according to a limited period of time (June–September 2020 and 2021). The research only shows an estimation of future tourist behaviour based on the variables of this study; it does not take into account the expected long-term future trends. Due to the high unpredictability and volatility of today's environment, research on future tourist behaviour should be more in-depth and comprehensive. Therefore, we recommend that investigations into the evolving situation in the tourism industry should continue in order to formulate development strategies to deal with new trends in tourist behaviour and to analyse unexpected consumer habits.

Notes

1 Monitor Deloitte, *Impact of the COVID-19 crisis on short- and medium-term consumer behavior. Will the COVID-19 crisis have a lasting effect on consumption?*, June 2020.
2 Dietrich A., Knotek E.S., Kuester K., Muller G.J., Ove R.C., Schoenle M.R., Weber M., Consumers and COVID-19: A real-time survey, Federal Reserve Bank of Cleveland, No. 8, 2020.
3 Chebli A., Said F., "The impact of Covid-19 on tourist consumption behaviour: A perspective article", *Journal of Tourism Management Research*, Vol. 7 No. 2, 2020, pp. 196–207.
4 Sheth J., "Impact of Covid-19 on consumer behavior: Will the old habits return or die?", *Journal of Business Research*, Vol. 117, 2020, pp. 280–283.
5 Sheth, J., op. cit.
6 Wachyuni, S.S., Kusumaningrum, D.A. 2020. "The effect of COVID-19 pandemic: How are the future tourist behavior?", *Journal of Education, Society and Behavioural Science*, Vol. 33 No. 4, 2020, pp. 67–76.
7 Monitor Deloitte, op. cit.
8 Chebli A., Said F., op. cit.

9 Wachyuni, S.S., Kusumaningrum, D.A., op. cit.
10 ISTAT, National Institute of Statistics, Viaggi e vacanze in Italia e all'estero, year 2019; 2020. https://www.istat.it/it/files/2020/02/RE-PORT_VIAGGIEVACANZE_2019.pdf
11 Monitor Deloitte, op. cit.
12 Gazzola P., Vătămănescu E.M., Andrei A.G., Marrapodi C., "Users' motivations to participate in the sharing economy: Moving from profits toward sustainable development", *Corporate Social Responsibility and Environmental Management*, Vol. 26 No. 4, 2019, pp. 741–751.

Conclusion

The shock of COVID-19 is currently the toughest stress test that the global economy has ever gone through. Since it is so extreme in both duration and severity, resilience must become a core philosophy within system management and operations to ensure organizations' ability to continue to function despite disruptions. Moreover, in addition to learning how to adapt and improve in the aftermath of crises, organizations must learn to seize upon new or revealed opportunities. This study explores the critical role of risk management and organizational resilience during times of adversity and turbulent crisis. Integrating concepts from risk management, Corporate Social Responsibility (CSR) and organizational resilience, this research proposes a conceptual framework to help organizations prepare for and respond to threats through agility and continuous learning capabilities.

The rapid spread of the novel coronavirus, COVID-19, since the first case occurred in December 2019 in Wuhan, Mainland China, resulted in significant and devastating impacts on the global economy, particularly for employment and especially in the tourism sector, where travel intentions changed in response to the necessary measures that were taken to contain the pandemic. This research aimed to identify and understand changes in tourists' consumption as a consequence of the COVID-19 outbreak, in order to predict how tourists will behave after the pandemic is over and to estimate how long it will take the tourism sector to recover. The research focuses specifically on tourism in Italy and takes into consideration the behaviour of tourists during the pandemic and after the start of containment measures (vaccines and the Green Pass). Although it is extremely difficult to predict the behaviour of tourism consumers after a crisis, an empirical study was conducted to understand tourists' sensitivity when faced with a health crisis like COVID-19. The goal was to identify any potential changes in travellers' consumption

DOI: 10.4324/9781003268963-6

as a consequence of the pandemic. Understanding fluctuating tourist behaviour can guide strategies and actions to provide adequate response measures to support the tourism industry's recovery.

This study was carried out through the administration of an online questionnaire, where a significant sample of Italian consumers participated in the survey, revealing insights about their intended behaviour and choices after the crisis. Based on quantitative and qualitative analysis, the results of the research indicate that the COVID-19 pandemic had and will continue to have an impact on travellers' behaviours and intentions in terms of personal safety, economic expenditure, confidence and attitude. It can be concluded that COVID-19 will influence travel habits, as people will avoid overcrowded destinations and prefer nearby destinations. The pandemic has also drawn attention to the issues of hygiene, cleanliness and health conditions in host destinations, which will become significant factors in future travel decisions. Consequently, faced with a worried clientele, tourism businesses (accommodation, catering, tourist attraction facilities, etc.) should further improve their hygiene conditions to regain the confidence of their visitors and send reassuring messages to guests who attach great importance to safety measures and hygiene standards. In this sense, it is also important that tourism managers focus on a media strategy that cultivates positive images and stimulates tourism during and after the COVID-19 crisis.

Current findings suggest that the dynamics of COVID-19 and its consequences present an unprecedented test of organizational resilience: stakeholders in the tourism industry need to be resilient, to adapt to shifts in consumptions, to fulfill their needs and to consider how to overcome all of the alarming predictions so that they can handle the crisis successfully and benefit from future growth. The COVID-19 shock is a major challenge that is so extreme in its duration and intensity that it is simply impossible to address it through absorptive capacities or a simple system adaptation; hence, the crisis should become an opportunity to progress and "bounce forward" through a combination of adaptation and transformation measures. As a consequence, this study is a mindful effort to enhance organizations' ability to develop a risk and resilience capacity so that they can react to unexpected events in ways that support the achievement of long-term sustainability and foster future success.

The conducted empirical study confirms that understanding consumers' beliefs and expectations is crucial for preparing to respond in the aftermath of a crisis like the COVID-19 pandemic. It's critical for companies to adapt quickly to new consumer behaviour and create a competitive advantage. To successfully survive, adapt, grow and compete, organizations should exhibit high resilience, constant and continuous learning, and immediate action. The analysis of the impact of COVID-19 on changing consumer needs confirms the theoretical claim that resilient organizations should possess some qualities. The study shows that only a combination of these qualities can lead organizations to be resilient in the long term. First of all, organizations must possess situational awareness of themselves, their stakeholders and the environment within which they act in order to be able to look for opportunities and respond to potential emergencies, to better understand future expectations and to develop the ability to accurately identify crises and their consequences. Furthermore, they should be capable of identifying and managing key vulnerabilities in order to avoid negative effects during a crisis situation and to assume an adaptive capacity that allows them to make decisions in a timely and appropriate way so that they can cope with unforeseen events. This study contributes to the existing theory by showing how important it is for organizations to better anticipate, prepare for, and build resilience for a future crisis, providing the system with the capacity for recovery and adaptation.

Learning to live with uncertainty, abandoning the notion of stability, expecting the unexpected, and increasing their capability to learn from crises is crucial for surviving in such a complex and volatile environment.

Because it is impossible to predict precisely what the future will look like after COVID-19, future studies could explore and investigate the evolving situation to formulate development strategies and deal with new and unexpected trends. Additionally, it will be important to build on the current research by collecting more evidence and empirical data to enrich our current understanding of the topic. Based on these conclusions, practitioners should explore how the capacity for resilience increases or decreases in organizations within a given time period so that management can start looking at resilience as an opportunity and a resource that needs to be enhanced over time. Among the innumerable uncertainties, doubts and ambiguities that the COVID-19 pandemic has plunged us all into, one outcome would seem undeniable: change is an inevitable feature of organizational life. Sometimes change is mandated by powerful external agents. Sometimes change is the natural consequence of interdependence and interaction. Sometimes change is a deliberate strategic initiative designed to increase competitive advantage. Regardless of the causal trigger, organizations must be able to efficiently and effectively alter their resources, competencies and business models in order to go beyond bouncing back and instead learn how to flourish in shifting conditions.

Index

Note: *Italic* page numbers refer to figures and page numbers followed by "n" denote endnotes.

Printed in the United States
by Baker & Taylor Publisher Services